ONE NATION UNDER GOD?

Christian Faith and
Political Action in America

ONE NATION UNDER GOD?

Christian Faith and Political Action in America

Mark A. Noll

1817

Harper & Row, Publishers, San Francisco

Cambridge, Hagerstown, New York, Philadelphia, Washington
London, Mexico City, São Paulo, Singapore, Sydney

Grateful acknowledgment is given for the use of the following: Letter from Stanhope Smith to Jonathan Dayton, December 22, 1801; Samuel Stanhope Smith Papers, 1 Box, folder 16. Letter from Elias Boudinot to Elisha Boudinot, January 7, 1801; Thorne Boudinot Collection, Box 1, folder 5. Published with the permission of Princeton University Library.

Unless otherwise noted, Scripture quotations contained herein are from the Revised Standard Version of the Bible, copyrighted 1946, 1952, 1971 by the Division of Christian Education of the National Council of the Churches of Christ in the U.S.A., and are used by permission. All rights reserved. The other Scripture translations used are the New International Version (NIV) and the King James Version (KJV).

FIRST EDITION

Library of Congress Cataloging-in-Publication Data

Noll, Mark A., 1946–
    One nation under God?

    Bibliography: p.
    Includes index.
    1. Church and state—United States—History.
2. United States—Church history. 3. Christianity and politics. I. Title.
BR516.N57 1988   261.7'0973   87-45715
ISBN 0-06-066303-0

88 89 90 91 92 HC 10 9 8 7 6 5 4 3 2 1

To
Tom Kay

Contents

Introduction

This book is about Christianity first, and only secondarily politics. It is a book about what religion has done to politics in America, but even more about what politics has done to religion. Its subject matter is largely historical, but it also intends to make a point for the present. The history deals with episodes in the nation's past when Christian believers, acting self-consciously as Christians, took an active interest in the course of political events. Study of these events is not irrelevant. For better and for worse, American Christians are Americans. A first step toward more responsible Christian action today, therefore, must be to understand American political activity in the past. That history of Christian political involvement is sometimes encouraging, sometimes discouraging, and often both at the same time. Although the episodes examined in this book are only a few of the many that could be studied, they provide more than enough matter for considering how the past may guide us in the present.

The book's point has to do with the relation between the kingdom of heaven and the kingdoms of this earth, between God and Caesar, between Christ and the nations. My contention is that for believers, the demands of the faith should always provide the framework for political action, rather than the reverse. Where circumstances allow Christians to influence the course of a nation's politics—as has been the case in the United States—politics can become an avenue for rendering service to God and to our fellow human beings. The values of Christianity can in fact strengthen a country. I will argue that Christian values have often served to strengthen this country. At the same time, the history of America also shows that Christian values do the most good for a nation when believers remember the difference between God's kingdom and their country, and also recall that only the Kingdom is forever.

Throughout the book, considerations of historical events are intermingled with suggestions concerning the proper character of Christian political practice. Yet its three major sections do concentrate on particular aspects of the theme.

THE SECTIONS OF THE BOOK

Part I treats two matters of perspective. Most importantly, it attempts to locate the central stream of American religion in the history of Christian interactions with culture. The fact that the characteristic Christian stance in America has been Protestant rather than Catholic, and that it has been Reformed Protestant rather than Lutheran or Anabaptist Protestant, is a matter of great significance. Why it makes so much difference for the relation of politics and religion is the question addressed in chapter 2.

Before tracing that Protestant history, however, the first chapter addresses a more immediately pressing issue: whether or in what sense the United States may be described as a "Christian nation" or a nation with a distinctive "Christian heritage." My position is that these terms are misleading if they are taken to mean a special divine blessing upon, or covenant with, the United States and its people as distinct from the peoples of other modern nations. On the other hand, if the terms are used simply to indicate that Christians have played central roles in the story of the nation and that Christian values have been important in the country's public life, they may be true in a carefully qualified sense. Chapter 1 provides only a sketch of the theological and historical considerations that lead to these conclusions, since I have in previous writings presented an extensive argument against the idea of a "Christian America" in the harder, more extreme understanding of the term.[1] I have not previously, however, explored at length the positive sense of America's Christian heritage. This book attempts that task. It does not pretend that Christian political involvement has been uniformly beneficial to the nation or to the church, yet it does show that the political actions of America's Christians have been helpful as well as harmful. Such actions have in fact testified to humility as well as to arrogance, to the guileless doing of good as well as to the ironic promotion of evil.

The book's second section explores political dimensions of America's Christian heritage by examining selected incidents from the nation's past. In them we observe intense Christian concern for the course of American public life and considerable involvement by Christians in political affairs. Although each of these historical episodes is a fit subject for a major study by itself, they must be treated briefly. Even so, they allow us to see where Christian convictions have made salient contributions to the development of a more just and equitable political order, as well as where they have hindered that development. An examination of these incidents also illustrates the way active political involvement has affected the church and its grasp of the Christian message. In the process we are afforded an excellent view of the particular strengths and weaknesses of America's characteristic "Reformed" approach to political action. And we see what it has meant for American Christians to pursue politics after the model of the religious revival. The historical episodes are taken mostly from the eighteenth and nineteenth centuries, but they include some of America's most important Christian politicians and some of the most conspicuous successes and failures of Christian political action.

I have tried to make these capsule histories as lively as possible for the sake of both believing and unbelieving readers. The intent throughout is to consider carefully the impact of Christian political activism both on public life and on religion; I hope, however, that the book can be useful to more than just the Christian community. In recent years sober analyses of religion in public life have been obscured by considerable misinformation and a generous misapplication of conventional wisdom.[2] To be sure, the light of history has its limits also. It can neither shine into all corners of the past nor do very much to illumine the years to come. Yet historical studies do provide means for overcoming the darkness of ignorance; reflection on history can prepare us to meet an uncertain future. To provide such light is the goal of the book's second section.

The final section returns once again to more general considerations. It summarizes main conclusions from the historical chapters and then proposes, on the basis of that history, a framework for Christian political involvement today. A separate chapter considers briefly the particular problems involved in putting the Bible to use in the political arena. The use of scriptural reasoning in politics is fraught with peril, as the nation's past amply illustrates, yet it is also essential both for religion and for the public good. If Christian political action is to retain its religious integrity *and* if it is to encourage justice and morality in public life (instead of self-interest disguised as religion), the Bible must be central. But it also must be used carefully and in accord with the central thrust of its own teaching.

THE QUESTIONS OF THE BOOK

Together, the book's three sections return often to several general questions that provide the occasion for the book's historical and religious evaluations:

(1) Why has the prevailing style of political action by American Christians been intuitive or a-theoretical? When faced with pressing political concerns, American Christians have tended to act first and ask questions later. What has been the result of such a tendency for political action and political reflection?

(2) What is the relationship between this direct and intuitive, or revivalistic, style of political action and the undoubted influence of Christianity in American political life? Is it in fact the case that Christian influence in public affairs is impossible without such a direct, wholehearted, and enthusiastic approach to politics?

(3) What good and what evil have resulted from the all-or-nothing strategies of Christian political action in America? How have these strategies affected political life, but, even more importantly, how have they affected the integrity of the Christian message itself?

(4) Is it possible to find examples of Christian political action that use a different approach from the characteristic all-or-nothing strategies? In other words, might Christian political action achieve more if it aimed at less? To use terms developed in a later chapter, what would happen if America's normal "Reformed" approach to political life were modified by by a "Lutheran" approach to the public sphere?

(5) Finally, how have American Christians used the Bible in politics? If such use reveals difficulties, what principles of biblical interpretation

and what elements of the Bible's contents need to be stressed for a healthier use of Scripture?

THE STANDPOINT OF THE AUTHOR: CHRISTIANITY AND POLITICS

These questions are the recurring points of reference in the pages that follow. Now, however, it is only fair to say a few words about my understanding of the central themes of the book, the Christian faith and the character of politics. For the first, I regard Christianity as a universal religion for all peoples in all times and places. The Scriptures and the traditions of the various Christian churches are relevant to the politics of a particular country, but only because their message concerns the salvation of individuals and groups from every nation. That message is the one with which Jesus opened his public ministry, as recorded in Mark 1:15—"The time is fulfilled, and the kingdom of God is at hand; repent, and believe in the gospel." It is the message that God has made himself known throughout human history, but especially in Jesus Christ, whose appearance on earth marked "the fullness of time." The divine revelation in Christ led to the creation of a Christian community, the Church, which exists to promote the kingdom of God, the standards of his law, and the message of his grace. The church is the home of those who have turned aside (or repented) from worshiping themselves and following the counsel of their own hearts to believing the good news (or gospel). That good news is preeminently the announcement that in and through Christ, God forgives sins and becomes to us a loving father. As it happens, I articulate the Christian faith with the accents of evangelical Protestantism, for that is my community of worship and theology. At the same time, I hope this understanding of Christian faith is generic enough to make the book useful for believers who are not evangelical Protestants as well as for nonbelievers and the uncommitted who are interested in a nonsectarian, yet still Christian, analysis of America's political history.

With most of the major Christian traditions, I look upon government as a human institution established by God for the good of humanity.[3] Government and the political process are instituted by God.

They have important, but limited, tasks. Politics and the state cannot exercise the functions of the family, nor are they meant to do the work of the church, nor is their end the salvation of humanity. Rather, the specific task of government—and the end of the political process—is to promote justice and prevent injustice, especially to the weaker members of a community.[4] In the modern West, Christian notions of justice extend to the conviction that all citizens be treated fairly, not just as individuals living under the authority of a state, but also as participants in the political process itself.

It is also fair at this point to say that, although I have strong personal positions on political questions, they are not easily aligned with the platforms of our two major parties. I have voted in five presidential elections, twice for the Republican candidate, twice for the Democratic, and once for an independent. I live in an Illinois county dominated by the Republican party and so, as a believer in the virtues of political competition, attempt to vote in local elections for competent Democrats as often as I can. Were I a resident of Chicago, I would do the same for Republicans.

A final introductory word pertains to the historical character of the book. Although I am writing as an "insider," as a Christian speaking first to other believers, I am also writing from my research as a professional historian. In that latter capacity I have attempted to be as faithful as possible in recounting the historical incidents. I do believe that Christian analysis of history is an important task in the church, but I do not presume to fathom the secrets of providence concerning the unraveling of American history.

These are general sketches of both my conception of Christianity and my politics. But they should be enough to suggest the point of view that underlies the analysis and judgments of the book.

Christian political thought and Christian political action may rise no higher than the thought and action of Jesus. In response to a devious question—"Tell us, then, what do you think? Is it lawful to pay taxes to Caesar, or not?"—posed in a charged political atmosphere (with those who opposed Rome and those who collaborated with Rome both eager to ensnare him), Jesus once offered an answer as simple as it was profound: "Render therefore to Caesar the things that are Caesar's, and to God the things that are God's" (Matt. 22:17–21). This book is about what believers have done in American history to render allegiance to God and to Caesar. It is also about maintaining the difference between the two, a task of discernment every bit as fateful in the late twentieth century as it was in the first.

I. PERSPECTIVE

1. A "Christian America"? No and Yes

Debates over the question of America's supposedly "Christian" character can resemble a boxing card without a main event. A few stout blows are delivered in preliminary bouts on lower order questions, yet even though everyone is shadowboxing furiously, a fully satisfying clash— in which opponents direct themselves primarily to each other rather than to their respective constituencies—rarely occurs.

To modern secularists the notion of a Christian America is absurd. Such people hold that the nation's founding documents—the Declaration of Independence and the Constitution—testify to a secular intent, whatever the private religious convictions of the founders might have been. In this view, the nation was established with a new kind of government, in which organized religion plays no role. Under the government of the United States, church and state are permanently (and gratifyingly) separate. Besides, these people say, the nation is now so pluralistic on religious and moral questions (not even to speak about its divisions on the possibility of knowing religious and moral truths) that only armed coercion could ever make America Christian.

Some religious conservatives contend with equal certainty that America was, and still may be, a Christian country. They see it as obvious that the first settlers came to these shores to worship freely and establish godly commonwealths. Equally obvious is the fact that America's great leaders have always encouraged the people to seek God in times of crisis. Do not even routine political pronouncements acknowledge God and the precepts of Christian morality? Is not American jurisprudence built self-consciously on the notion of a "higher law," or divine principles of justice offering a general framework for all legislation and regulation? And has not divine providence manifestly preserved the nation from its enemies and given it unprecedented prosperity and influence in the world? So runs the thinking of Christian traditionalists.

ADJUDICATION THROUGH HISTORY AND THEOLOGY

The common feature of these contrasting views is that neither has much time for careful study of the past. In the first case, bare phrases from the Constitution or later court decisions are translated into wide-ranging political principles confirming America's secular character. In the second, bold assertions from early American leaders become proofs of providential action establishing the unique religious destiny of the country. To neither case, however, is history really important. The ability to find the proper quotations from earlier generations—without context, without evaluation, without understanding—is the key.

A better way is to understand past events in context. History as it was lived, rather than as we would like it to have unfolded, must be the place to start a consideration of Christian America. Moreover, examining past events with care and with sensitivity to their moral implications is a task at which both believers and unbelievers can work together, at least to some degree. Historical study, in short, is one way to stimulate helpful discussion of an emotional theme.

For Christians, a second element will greatly aid the inquiry. That element is theological reasoning, which, in this case, must be distinguished from providential reasoning. Theology grows from the Christian community's listening to the Bible and to its reflection on both Christian traditions and modern circumstances. Traditional Christian theology certainly includes a belief in providence—that God is perpetually active in sustaining the world and especially involved in spreading the Christian message. But traditional theology also includes a built-in suspicion of presumptuous claims to fathom providence, to know the mind of God. False prophets claim to speak for God and see the world as God sees it. True prophets point to the divine words of Scripture and the church's long history of reflection on those words.

The distinction between theological reasoning and providential reasoning yields a very important practical difference in understanding the history of America. A providential approach claims to know what God was doing at any one time or place in the outworking of the nation's history. Thus, Puritans believed that Indians destroyed white settlements in 1675 because the English settlers had been neglecting the Sabbath. Some Northern Christians felt the South lost the Civil War as a divine judgment on the immorality of slavery. More recently, some Christians have expressed the opinion that the national crime rate rose because the Supreme Court banned prayer in the public schools. These statements may be correct, or they may be incorrect. No one, except God, knows. But God has not chosen to reveal his mind on these events.

What God did choose to reveal were his precepts and a record of his actions in Scripture. And God has also chosen to provide an unbroken succession of students and interpreters of those Scriptures and of the church's traditions that grew out of them. From these theological resources we may indeed learn much that is relevant to American history: for example, that warfare arises from sinful greed and pride (James 4:1); that the American form of racial chattel slavery violated principles of personal integrity as well as economic justice (Jer. 7:6); or that practices of personal morality affect the well-being of a society (the Book of Judges). Unlike providential reasoning, however, theology does not give us an instant analysis of the past. Rather, it provides principles with which the past can be evaluated. In turn, that evaluation—along with careful examination of historical events, statements, and circumstances—gives us a place to begin a consideration of America's Christian character.

THE RECENT SEARCH FOR CHRISTIAN AMERICA

Modern attention to the question of America's Christian character arises from a combination of historical celebrations and contemporary political developments. The public ceremonies surrounding the bicentennial of the Declaration of Independence (1976), the centennial renovation of the Statue of Liberty (1986), and the bicentennial of the Constitution (1987) have directed an unusual amount of public attention to the nation's founding era. One of the most obvious features of that era was its commonplace belief in God and ready acceptance of traditional moral teachings. Americans who have read about the early development of the United States know that not all the founding fathers were zealous, orthodox Christians. Yet it is no secret that even leaders like Benjamin Franklin and Thomas Jefferson, who abandoned traditional forms of Christian belief, were comfortable with both religious language (like Jefferson's phrases about "nature's God," the "Creator," and "Divine Providence" in the Declaration of Independence) and religious practice (like Franklin's suggestion at a precarious moment during the Constitutional Convention that the delegates pause to pray for divine guidance).[1] This kind of historical information, along with the awareness that other founding fathers were more traditionally Christian, has encouraged the conviction that the work of that generation amounted to an achievement with profound religious implications.

A further stimulus to the idea of Christian America has been the effective political lobbying of activistic theological conservatives, often styled the New Right, or the New Christian Right. Quite apart from their desire to advance specific policy proposals, leaders of this movement are also driven by an image of the past. They feel that the nation once was better than it now is. They hold that Christian values once prevailed widely in the country as the stuff of private life and the organizing coordinates of the political sphere; then, through a series of unfortunate occurrences, anti-Christian forces gained strength and over the last century have conspired to attack Christian influence and rewrite the history of the country in secular terms. Nonetheless, most of these leaders urge, it is still not too late. If the country's religious sector comes to its senses, if the nation as a whole repents of its wrongs, if traditional morality once against prevails, then God will renew his blessings upon the land and restore the moral character and religious fervor that has been lost.

PATRIOTISM VERSUS AMERICAN CHRISTIAN PATRIOTISM

It is important to note that the discussion of Christian America does not revolve around the issue of simple patriotism as such. Throughout all of human history a special attachment to the native place has broadened out into a more general love for the homeland. In the modern world that attachment to native place has been expressed through powerful rituals and time-tested structures. These include slogans ("God save the Queen!"), songs ("O Canada, our home and native land"), pledges ("to the flag, and to the republic for which it stands"), as well as beloved historical traditions.

The Christian Scriptures seem simply to take for granted the basic attachment to our native places. It was second nature for Old Testament writers to identify Israelites by tribe, thus testifying to bonds of both geography and history. Almost as instinctively, New Testament authors called individuals by their place of birth, "Saul of Tarsus" or "Joseph of Arimathea." Beyond this, numerous biblical passages mandate loyalty to political institutions. God has established the ruling powers that be (Rom. 13:1–7). Prayer should be offered for heads of state and other civic officials (1 Tim. 2:1–2). Ceasar deserves his due (Mark 12:17). These references only confirm that patriotism, loyalty to one's own place, is a path of nature that also accords with biblical norms.

The question of patriotism in America, however, is much more complicated than the question of patriotism in general. Throughout its history our nation has enjoyed the presence of many influential groups of Christians. For over three hundred years believers have tried in various ways to construct their public and private lives in accord with Scripture. And many of these efforts have been successful, at least in the eyes of those who made the effort. When modern believers observe this history, the temptation is strong to make another claim, that American structures of government and patterns of economic organization approximate ideals given by God in Scripture.

In light of the conspicuous Christian presence in American history, some believers have even concluded that the story of our land is in some sense an extension of the history of salvation. The Puritans did indeed feel that God had established a special covenant with their New World settlements, and so it must be that the United States continues as a nation in special covenant with God. The United States did indeed win its independence from Great Britain against considerable odds; therefore, some say, God must have providentially intervened in that conflict on the side of "his people," the Americans. And so, for them, America today must still be an anointed land, set apart by a divine plan for an extraordinary existence as a nation and an extraordinary mission to the world.

With these views, patriotic loyalty to America becomes more than the common affection that all peoples naturally exercise toward their native land. It is a special interpretation of divine providence and a transformation of national allegiance into a statement about the mind of God. It may be called the strong, or exalted, view of Christian America.

THEOLOGY AND HISTORY AGAINST THE STRONG VIEW OF CHRISTIAN AMERICA

In the face of theological reasoning and a careful consideration of the past, this strong view of the notion of Christian America is misguided at best, pernicious at worst. In the first instance, the Bible is very clear about the status of nations. Only one nation in the history of the world has enjoyed divine favor, in its status as a nation, and that was Old Testament Israel. Standard Christian teaching holds, moreover, that Old Testament Israel enjoyed its special status as "chosen nation" in order to prepare the entire world for the reception of God's saving grace. After the full revelation of God's glory in Christ, "God's country" was made up of believers "from every tribe and tongue and people and nation" (Rev. 5:9).

No nation, including the United States, can be God's "new Israel." Much else may be said about the relative good and evil that has been accomplished by Americans and in America, but it is in fact idolatry to think that our nation has received those special dispensations that Scripture declares God has reserved for the Church. The consequences of this theological conclusion are plain. Patriotic loyalties—whether to "the land of the free and the home of the brave," to Mother Russia, or to any other country—are always subordinate to a Christian's first loyalty. And that highest loyalty is to the "nation" of those who have turned in faith to Christ.

The New Testament mandates political loyalty to properly constituted governments. At the same time, it subordinates that loyalty to higher allegiances. The apostles use stronger language to describe loyalty to the Church (Gal. 3:27–28), to humanity in general (Acts 17:26), and even to the family (1 Tim. 4:8) than they do for loyalty to country. Christians who honor the teaching of the Bible on theological or religious matters should follow its lead here also. However important loyalty to government, nation, economic system, or particular culture might be, that loyalty may never compromise a Christian's higher loyalties to the communion of saints, the universal scope of humanity, or (under normal circumstances) the family.

Historical investigation leads to the same conclusions as theological reasoning does. Although great good has been done in America from Christian motives (the subject of much of the rest of this book), the nation has also been the scene of great evil, often in the name of Christ. If we really believed the notion of a special manifestation of divine benevolence to America, we would end with a twisted view of God. It is beyond belief, for example, that God would have ordained by a special providence that European colonists should treat native Americans—human beings made in God's image for whom Christ died—like the beasts of the field. It is equally beyond belief that a special providential act would create or sanction America's system of black racial slavery, with its monumental injustices. It is almost equally incredible that God expressly sanctioned the exploitation of labor and the damage to the environment that has been part of America's economic history. (This is not a comment on the system of free-market capitalism, which, in my judgment, is potentially compatible with Christian principles; it is a judgment on the practices in economic relationships in the nation's history.) These examples are not meant to say that the destructive events in American history proceeded outside the control of providence; it is to suggest that a providential interpretation of history that features a special divine covenant with the United States leads to very awkward conclusions. (See appendix A for a consideration of other modern nations that also feel they are in covenant with God.)

A WEAK VERSION OF CHRISTIAN AMERICA?

If we set aside the notion that America has enjoyed a unique relationship with God, it still may be possible to talk about "Christian America" in a different sense. Let us admit that the United States is not messianic, that its history is not a part of the history of salvation. Let us also grant that the first loyalty of Christians on earth is to the church and that, because of Christian principles, humanity as a whole is more important than that segment of humanity residing in any particular nation. Might it still not be possible to conclude that the governmental structures and political institutions of some nations come closer to embodying principles in accord with the general norms of the Bible than those of other nations? Might not the histories of some nations reveal clearly the beneficial effects of faithful Christians putting their religion into practice? Might not the assumptions about human nature and divine providence in some political systems come closer to standards of God's kingdom than others? And might not the actions of certain nations at certain times be more important than those of other nations for the benefit of all humanity, as the Christian traditions define that benefit?

At least in theory, the answer to all these questions is yes. By reasoning from theological principle and historical actuality—rather than from intuitions about God's secret providence—it should be possible to say that some aspects of a nation's history comport better with generally Christian principles than do other aspects of that history.

Thus, in the case of the United States, certain features of the national history stand out as exemplary, from the angle of Christian interpretation. At their best, the nation's traditions of democratic liberty fit well with biblical teachings on the dignity of all people under God. In living memory, the United States was a key factor in liberating Europe and Asia from the tyranny of the Axis powers. Americans have played a large role in the modern missionary movement that has taken the gospel to millions around the world. And many people from other lands still look to America, and with considerable justice, as a promised land of economic, political, and religious freedom.

For each of these cases, and others besides, it is possible to reason that on the basis of sound theological principles, a given event or situation may have been "Christian," or at least in reasonable conformity to Christian norms. In this restricted sense, American Christians may be justified in thinking of their country—in certain respects and at certain periods—as a "Christian nation."

QUALIFYING THE WEAK VIEW OF CHRISTIAN AMERICA

At the same time, any conclusions about a "Christian America" on these terms must remain open to challenge and modification. In the first instance, these kinds of conclusions represent the last stage in a chain of reasoning. If we have misinterpreted the historical circumstance or if we have misapplied the theological principle, then our conclusion about the Christian character of an event or situation must be revised. Conclusions about "Christian America" in this weak form are inferences from our own reasoning, not revelations from God.

Second, the conclusion that God has blessed America in unusual ways cannot be based primarily on the nation's material prosperity or its military might. In Scripture, the Babylonians, the Syrians, and the Assyrians had much more powerful armies than the Hebrews. The Apostle Paul said he knew the hand of the Lord more certainly in peril than he did in prosperity. Since the whole message of Christianity hangs on the self-abasement and weakness of the Cross, it would be odd indeed for Christians to equate divine blessing simply with material prosperity.

Third, a conclusion that the nation has come close to Christian norms in some circumstances and situations should not shut off consideration of those times and places in which national policy has moved in an evil direction. Much good has taken place in America, but also much evil. The list is long enough to give anyone pause. It includes the effective genocide of the native Americans, the enslavement of blacks (with the man-stealing, family destroying, and dehumanization so manifestly condemned in Scripture), the twentieth-century promotion of materialistic consumerism, fire bombings of civilians in World War II, political misjudgments and military atrocities in the Vietnam conflict, and more. Whatever we may conclude about the Christian character of the United States, we may never forget the scandals for which the nation is also responsible.

Finally, conclusions about the Christian character of American history and institutions must always be subject to alternative deductions from Scripture and alternative inferences from history. Mennonites and some other Christians, for example, believe that biblical teaching prohibits all participation in warfare by believers. Anyone who concludes that God "blessed" America in an unusual way through warfare owes it to other Christians like the Mennonites to reexamine the theological and historical reasoning undergirding such a conclusion.

On a different level, black Americans who still experience the destructive effects of slavery and systematic national discrimination may not come to the same conclusions about God and the nation as their white fellow citizens do. They may argue that a biblical assessment of history shows the United States to be as exploitative as other societies and so in no real sense a Christian nation.

Christians must tolerate—and encourage—these divergent interpretations of American history. Alternative applications of theological principle to historical circumstances can only sharpen our efforts to understand and evalute the nation's history. Even when discussions of this sort lead to disagreement over the Christian character of America, they are profitable. They are a reminder that conclusions about Christian America, even in this weak sense, are human inferences rather than divine revelation. And they help the Christian to recall that ultimate loyalty belongs to the church, where divergent theological interpretations are a constant stimulus, rather than to the nation, where claims of ultimate loyalty are a constant temptation to idolatry.

In the rest of this book we examine historical events and episodes in the light of theological principle. This approach offers a series of test cases for the possibility that America has been a Christian nation in the weak sense of the term.

More important, however, the book hopes to show the strengths and weaknesses of Christian political action in itself. If we can reach that goal, then whatever conclusions are drawn about the historical character of America as a Christian nation, believers may be better equipped to act politically today.

The question of "Christian America" in the end is a metaphysical question. Nothing essential is won or lost if we put off answering it. The question of Christian political action, on the other hand, is a practical issue of pressing consequence. Much more important than knowing what God thinks of America is knowing what type of action lives up to the standards of his kingdom. For the question of Christian America, we are in the same situation as Abraham Lincoln was when he was asked to join in prayer that God would favor the Northern side in the Civil War. Lincoln's response was that, although this might be an acceptable prayer, it was much more important that Northerners pray to be on *God's* side.

The place to begin a consideration of the political behavior of American Christians, however, is not with the incidents and episodes themselves; it is with a more general consideration of how the main characteristics of Christian political behavior in America fit the general pattern of Christian involvement with culture. For that purpose, the history of Christianity before the European settlement of North American becomes vitally important.

2. The American Christian Heritage as a "Reformed" Tradition

The course of religious involvement in American politics was set before there was an America. Even before English settlers in the early seventeenth century established the colonies that would one day become the United States, the dominant American pattern of religious-political interaction was firmly in place. Through nearly four centuries, that pattern has remained relatively constant. The players have changed; the rules have shifted to favor now one group of competitors, now another; triumphs and defeats on issues unforeseeable by the first generation have occurred; the playing field has been renovated many times, so much so that it hardly resembles its seventeenth-century shape at all; but the game remains the same. It remains the same, moreover, not just for Christians seeking to influence political life, but also for "post-Christians," or secularists, who have set aside the content of traditional religion but nonetheless maintain habits of thought about public life arising directly from the Protestant Reformation.

Several historical circumstances explain this pattern of religious-political involvement and its long-standing power in America. One is the chronology of the Protestant Reformation. Another has to do with contrasts among the leading forms of Protestantism. Yet a third involves alternative patterns of religious-political engagement that though present in the history of Christianity have not exerted much influence in America. It is necessary to show how a stance toward politics that developed in Christian Europe in the sixteenth century could survive in the New World even after the Americanization of European religious habits and, later, the secularization of American public life. A consideration of these historical circumstances may seem to carry us far afield from the course of religion and politics in the United States; in fact, however, they are key ingredients for revealing what America's Christian heritage has meant, and not meant, for political life in the United States.

THE DIRECTION OF THE REFORMATION IN ENGLAND

It is well known that Martin Luther, pioneered the movement that eventually became the Protestant Reformation. Luther's Ninety-Five Theses of 1517 called for a renewed understanding of repentance and faith. His great tracts of 1520, including the attack on the Catholic sacramental system in his *Babylonian Captivity of the Church*, fleshed out the major principles that almost all Protestants would come to share: justification by faith, the priesthood of all believers, and the supremacy of Scripture as religious authority. By the end of the 1520s, Luther had translated the New Testament into German (and so opened the Scriptures to the people as a whole), published his catechism and several plans for renewing the life of local congregations (and so laid the foundation for Protestant forms of spirituality), and also led the reorganization of churches in the lands of his Saxon prince (and so shifted matters of church authority from the Catholic hierarchy to German territorial rulers). All this occurred while England, Scotland, Switzerland, France, Holland, and other centers of later Protestant growth were still predominantly within the orbit of Roman Catholicism.

In England, a desire for reform existed on two levels during the first three decades of the sixteenth century.[1] A few academics, mostly with some connection to the colleges of Cambridge University, and widely scattered pockets of common folk, sometimes with historical connections to the Lollard movement of John Wycliffe, yearned for spiritual reform of the English church. The break from the Catholic church came not from these sectors, however, but from King Henry VIII's wish to manage his own marriage free from the authority of the papacy. While Lutheran books and practices were exerting a covert influence in England, Henry's desire for a divorce from Catherine of Aragon led to the rupture with Rome. Throughout the 1530s Henry maintained a conservative stance on religious matters, even as he proceeded to remove the pope's influence from the church in England. At the same time, reformers more interested in spiritual life than civil authority were busy adapting Lutheran convictions for the English people. Thomas Cranmer, who would later compile the Book of Common Prayer, studied the work of Lutheran theologians with great care and even married the niece of a Lutheran pastor. William Tyndale, the translator of Scripture into English, moved in Luther's orbit for many years and imitated several aspects of Luther's German Bible in his own translation. It would be too much to say that the Englishmen eager for spiritual reform in the 1530s were Lutherans in a precise sense of the term, yet it was true that Luther's influence was as strong or stronger than that of any other theologian in England at the time.

This situation began to change at the death of Henry VIII in 1547. Henry's sickly son, who became King Edward VI upon his father's death, had been given a Protestant education. Although he was only nine years old when he assumed the throne, he was determined to carry through a Protestant reform of spirituality and church practice. During Edward's brief reign, 1547–1553, however, Protestant influences from the Continent became quite diverse. Some English reformers continued to read Luther, but others were more drawn to the example of Martin Bucer in Strasbourg, Heinrich Bullinger in Zurich, or the young John Calvin in Geneva. In the great church documents that Thomas Cranmer prepared under Edward VI—the first and second Books of Common Prayer and the Forty-two Articles (which were later revised to become the famous Thirty-nine Articles of the Church of England)—Lutheran emphases were mingled thoroughly with those of other Protestant reformers.

When Edward VI died in 1553, he was succeeded by his older sister, Mary (the daughter of Catherine of Aragon). Mary was a devout Catholic who was determined to right the wrongs done by both her father (she would return the English church to the papacy) and by her brother (she would recall the Church of England to Catholic practices). It therefore came to pass that the leaders of England's Reformation found their nation a very dangerous place in those years. Some 290 Protestants, including Thomas Cranmer, went to the stake as martyrs to their cause. Others were able to lie low in England and continue an underground Protestant life. Still others, including many of the most important Protestant leaders, sought refuge on the Continent. These exiles included some of the men who had taken the most aggressive steps toward pushing English church life in a Protestant direction. Of course they could not know it in 1553 and 1554, but their number also included many of the figures who would set the course for English Protestantism after Mary's death in 1558.

It is precisely this juncture in the history of the English Reformation—still several decades before the first permanent settlements in America (Jamestown, Virginia, in 1607; Plymouth and Boston, Massachusetts, in 1620 and 1630)—that became so important for the later course of religion and politics in America. Until this time, the English Reformation was a fairly thorough mixture of Lutheran influences, elements from other Protestant leaders in Europe, and native English proclivities. When English Protestants fled their native land during the reign of Catholic Queen Mary, however, they did not go to the lands of Luther: northern Germany or Scandinavia. They went instead to regions controlled by Reformed or (in a very broad use of the term) "Calvinist" Protestants. Many of them ended up in Calvin's Geneva. Additional refugees found a home in other Reformed cities in southwestern Germany.

For a number of reasons Lutheran lands were virtually closed to the English Protestant refugees. Following the death of Martin Luther in 1546 internal theological strife had torn his movement, both over who would emerge as successor to the great leader and over several troubling theological issues. At the same time, the Lutheran lands suffered political and military reverses in their struggle with the Holy Roman Emperor Charles V (a fervent Catholic who, among his many other influential kinships, was the nephew of Catherine of Aragon). Divided religiously by doctrinal and personal strife, weakened politically by defeat at the hand of the emperor, Lutheran Europe was in no position to offer a place of refuge for exiles from England.

The situation was quite different in the areas dominated by Reformed Protestantism. Calvin had secured a thoroughly Protestant Reformation in Geneva early in the 1550s and welcomed the English with open arms. He put churches and schools at their disposal and even offered assistance for translators seeking to refine and expand Tyndale's earlier translation of the Bible (the work that emerged, the Geneva Bible, was the most influential English translation of Scripture until the appearance of the King James Bible over fifty years later). The welcome in Strasbourg, Frankfurt, and other cities under Reformed, in contrast to Lutheran, control was equally warm.

Most of the English refugees returned to their native land in 1558 or shortly thereafter, when the Catholic Mary died and was succeeded by her sister Elizabeth. Elizabeth was no ardent Protestant, yet she clearly cast her lot in that direction, and so it was once again safe for the leaders of England's earlier Reformation to return home. When they did so, they came back to England with positive impressions of their Reformed and Calvinistic hosts and of the reforms they were attempting in their cities and lands. John Knox, the Scottish reformer who had earlier contributed to Protestant efforts in England, said of Calvin's Geneva that it was "the most perfect school of Christ that ever was in the earth since the days of the Apostles."[2] Other Britons did not express their enthusiasm so extravagantly, but the warm welcome they had received from European Calvinists exerted a great influence on their own attitudes toward Christian belief and practice.

The result was that the more advanced or "thorough" English Protestants strove for the same sort of reforms in England that they had witnessed on the Continent. And what they had seen primarily was energetic, wholehearted efforts to reshape all of life in accordance with Reformed understandings of the Bible. At least for these more self-conscious Protestants, England's earlier theological eclecticism was not enough. It was necessary to pursue a Reformation that was thoroughly Reformed.

The long-term ramifications of this historical episode have been immense. Reformed models from the Continent were especially important for the English Puritans as they struggled for a further reformation of England and its church. The Puritans, who had arisen by the 1580s as a semi-organized movement, aimed at subjecting all of life to God. They would, by God's grace, tame the sinfulness of the self. They would complete the reform of the Church of England by conforming its doctrine and practices to Scripture. And they would so preach and live the gospel as to make all England a land of righteousness and peace. These aspirations, which amounted to an English adaptation of motives they had experienced first hand in Reformed Europe, drove the English Puritans from their first emergence in the 1570s and 1580s through the time of Oliver Cromwell's dominance in the 1640s and 1650s.

These were also the aspirations that inspired the Puritans who came to America in the decades following 1630. When events in England during the first third of the seventeenth century seemed to rule out the achievement of Puritan purposes in that land, a significant minority of Puritans came to the New World. Here they would establish godly commonwealths where the reform of self, church, and society could go forward and where England itself could find a workable pattern for its own thorough reformation. The actual course of events in America proved more ambiguous than the Puritan immigrants had anticipated. They never were able to inspire much emulation in England or to completely satisfy themselves that a thorough reform had been carried out in America. Nonetheless, the Reformed ideas that they brought with them as Puritans from England to America determined the early history of New England, exerted a compelling influence elsewhere in the American colonies, and became the dominant force in the shaping of religious attitudes toward public life in American civilization.

In this way it came about that although Lutheranism was the first Protestantism and America has been strongly influenced by Protestantism, American civilization owes almost nothing specifically to the influence of Luther.

REFORMED AND LUTHERAN: THEOLOGY

On narrow theological grounds, it means very little that American Protestantism has been Puritan and Reformed rather than Lutheran. To be sure, Lutherans and Calvinists have a long history of theological strife, dating back to acerbic debates during the lifetime of Martin Luther over the meaning of the Lord's Supper. Other theological issues, like the precise character of the divine and human natures in Christ's one person, or God's intention for those who do not become Christians, have also divided Lutherans and the Reformed. Yet in the universe of possible Christian beliefs, the Lutherans and the Calvinists stand quite close to each other. Not only do they share the basic Protestant convictions about justification, the Scriptures, and the priesthood of all believers with other Protestants, both are also deeply indebted to the theological tradition stemming from Augustine (354–430). Lutherans and Calvinists say very similar things about the weaknesses of sinful human nature. They both exalt the power of God and the work of Christ as the central matters in human salvation. In addition, they both understand the Bible as a book unified by God's promises to rescue an undeserving humanity. And both are traditionalists on the sacraments, believing not only in the continued validity of infant baptism, but also that baptism and the Lord's Supper are more than merely symbols of God's goodness (they are genuine indications of his "real presence"). On all these matters, and many others, the Lutherans and the Reformed stand together and are divided from most other Protestants.

The great significance in the fact that Calvinists rather than Lutherans shaped early American culture does not, therefore, lie in theology as such; rather, the crucial differences are found in contrasting attitudes toward culture, toward life in the world.

REFORMED AND LUTHERAN: LIFE IN THE WORLD

Unlike their theological differences, the differences between Lutherans and the Reformed on cultural matters were large and important. To oversimplify a complicated picture, we may draw attention to the three critical relationships in any Christian system: (1) the relation between God and his people (as individuals and the church), (2) between the church and the world, and (3) between God and the world. For Lutherans, the first and third relationship belong to two different spheres. God has created two different "swords" or "kingdoms" through which to exercise his will. To individuals as spiritual beings God works through the church; to individuals as members of society God works through established governments, economic systems, and social structures. The second relationship (between the church and the world) does provide a way for God's saving will to moderate and influence activities in the world, but the center of spiritual renewal will always be firmly located in the relationship between God and the individual in the church. By contrast, the Reformed have traditionally seen all three relationships in close harmony. God calls people to himself, incorporates them into the church, and then through the church works to transform the wider world for his glory. The differences between the two approaches are not absolute, but they are important.

In the concerns of Luther and Calvin themselves we can see the difference made by degrees of emphasis.[3] However much attention Luther gave to practical holiness of life, the center of his thought remained the cross of Christ. However much Calvin preached the cross, his message constantly returned to the practicalities of holy living. On the level of polity these differences in tone and tendency grew even more important. Luther was relatively indifferent to questions of church order because he knew how easily ecclesiastical propriety became spiritual pride. Calvin acknowledged the same possibility, yet poured great energies into creating a truly godly church. Luther counseled restraint in matters political. It was better to suffer injustice from the state than to allow a passion for political reform to obscure the desperate condition of every human (ruler or ruled, tyrant or reformer) before the righteousness of God. Calvin never abandoned the centrality of Jesus (it was Calvin who popularized the picture of Christ as prophet, priest, and king), but he thought that the reform of politics was an activity that Christians, grateful to God for the gift of salvation, should pursue as part of the drive for holiness.

A forceful illustration of these differences concerns what theologians call "the third use of the law." Traditionally, God's law was thought to have three purposes: first, to act as a holy standard showing individuals how desperately they need to find salvation in Christ; second, to serve as a general guideline for the ordering of life in the world; and third, to show Christians (now rescued from "the curse of the law") the kind of life that God would have them lead. In point of fact, both Luther and Calvin taught all three "uses" of the law. But Luther laid much greater emphasis on the way the law reduced human pride and prepared the way for the mercy shown to humanity in Christ than he did on the way the law offered guidelines for practical living to the

Christian. Calvin, on the other hand, though he never denied that God's law was vitally important to drive people to God, also developed at great length the implications of the law for Christians. W. Fred Graham has nicely summarized the practical results of this contrast:

Calvin's message had a [social] impact even stronger than that of his spiritual father Luther. Luther felt God's law primarily as the threat which drives us to God's mercy, and that was the end of its Lutheran usefulness. For Calvin, the law had a further purpose, that of guiding the believer after he had accepted God's mercy and forgiveness. This meant that the Calvinist was a more "driven" Christian—driven to a life more in harmony with stern biblical morality, and thus driven also to change society in this direction. This helps explain why Calvin was more concerned than Luther to tell soldiers how they must fight—no rape, pillage, or harassment of noncombatants—and also more concerned to tell the Geneva city Council how it should govern. Luther turned over such legal questions to the political arm, and this in so small measure helped produce in Germany and Scandinavia a more peaceful, less revolutionary movement, when compared with the government-toppling cadres issuing from Geneva.[4]

In sum, from their relatively similar theological standpoints, Luther and Calvin developed significantly different approaches to life in the world, differences that those in the broadly Lutheran and broadly Reformed sections of Protestantism have tended to observe.

PURITAN, THEN EVANGELICAL, THEN SECULAR AMERICA

In America it has made all the difference that Reformed rather than Lutheran attitudes toward culture have prevailed. In terms of the nation's religious life, we have indeed seen major changes. For the sake of simplicity it is possible to differentiate three quite distinct periods in our history—the colonial period under the influence of the Puritans (roughly 1630 to the time of the American Revolution), the national period under a more generally evangelical influence (roughly 1776 to the last third of the nineteenth century), and a modern period under the sway of the secular (roughly the last century). Yet in each one, the general approach to the formation of culture has been the same. A word about these three periods is in order before we describe that similarity.

The Puritan period was a time when European Calvinism, though not the only religion in the colonies, was the dominant influence. Whether English Puritans in New England, Scottish Presbyterians or the Dutch and German Reformed in the middle colonies, or a Church of England with a distinctly Reformed cast in the South, the tone was set by European immigrants who had been strongly influenced by Reformed patterns of theology and life. Immigrants to America tended to be less traditional than those left behind in Europe, yet they did not innovate dramatically in religion. Hierarchy was still the norm in the churches. Though congregations might have a role in selecting their clergymen, they were expected to listen silently and with respect as these learned gentlemen brought the word of the Lord. Divine sovereignty and the mystery of divine action were still the heart of theology; God moved in mysterious ways that required humble and dutiful submission from his people.

The message of democracy and self-sufficiency of the Revolutionary era altered the theological and practical character of American religion. The War for American Independence, and even more "the democratization of mind" that accompanied it, led to a rapid Americanization of the nation's religion.[5] Traditional Reformed emphases on divine sovereignty in salvation and divine direction of the church (through the powerful ministerial elite) could not survive the winds of revolution. Theologies stressing human free will replaced theologies that emphasized predestination; church order based on the voluntary activity of individual members replaced churches organized by a hierarchy of appointed officials. With Methodists in the vanguard, many other new denominations (e.g., Disciples, Free Will Baptists, "Christian," Mormons) close behind, and a period of rapid reorientation by the older denominations (Congregationalists, Presbyterians, Episcopalians), the nineteenth century became, in the words of Sydney Ahlstrom, "the golden day of democratic evangelicalism."[6]

The revival, with its dependence upon charismatic leadership and its intensely popular style, was now the norm for church expansion. Its approach to religion was so powerful that it spilled over, as we will soon see, to other areas of American life. The voluntary society, with its reliance upon energetic laypeople and its *ad hoc* approach to social issues, set the standard pattern for church action in the world.

"Evangelical America" came to an end sometime toward the close of the nineteenth century. To be sure, evangelical impulses remained very strong, and evangelical churches of almost every possible description remained a dynamic part of the national landscape. But the domination of evangelical Protestantism in American life was over. The restructuring of the nation's social and economic existence—from farm and village to city, from small-scale economic exchange to the industrial and merchandising revolutions—forever altered the base within which evangelicalism had flourished. Mass migrations brought millions to America who did not fit comfortably into the culture developed by the Protestants of British descent. Scandinavian and German Lutherans, Roman Catholics from Ireland and central Europe, Orthodox Christians from Russia and Greece, Jews from eastern Europe, a good number of immigrants with no religious affiliation, and eventually the Asian adherents of Eastern religions strained the evangelical hegemony of antebellum America to and beyond the breaking point. In addition, a major restructuring of the nation's intellectual life moved the educated elite of the country beyond the certainties of Protestant Christianity. For many in the universities, where graduate schools and a new professional spirit came to prevail at the end of the nineteenth century, the writings of Darwin, Marx, and Freud seemed more relevant than the message of the Bible and the traditions of the churches. For a growing number of common people outside the circles of the educated elite, traditional Christianity became just as irrelevant. The result was a nation in which several religions flourished—traditional evangelical Protestantism, Roman Catholicism of several ethnic varieties, other Christian and non-Christian religions—at the same time that largely a- or even anti-religious assumptions exercised their sway as the arbiters of America's intellectual and cultural life.

POLITICAL CONTINUITY AND RELIGIOUS DISCONTINUITY

The key matter for our purposes, however, is not how much the nature of America's religious life has changed over the centuries, but how much attitudes toward public life, and especially politics, have remained the same. The dominant pattern of American political involvement has always been one of direct, aggressive action. Like the early leaders of Calvinism on the Continent and like the English Puritans, Americans have moved in a straight line from personal belief to social reform, from private experience to political activity. For the colonial Puritans and the nineteenth-century evangelicals this meant mounting religious crusades. Puritans and evangelicals assumed it was necessary to move directly from passion for God and the Bible to passion for the renovation of society. The most recent, secular period of American life has been no less characterized by crusading zeal. Now, however, it is not so much zeal for God and the Bible as infatuation with science and technique, solicitude for American influence among the nations, or a passion for private rights that fuel the efforts to renovate society. The common strategy in each period has been whole-hearted pursuit of political goals defined on the basis of private religious belief (or in the secular period, other private beliefs functioning as once religion functioned). The public sphere, which increasingly has meant the realm of government, exists as a forum in which to promote the virtues defined by the individual's religion (or substitute religion). In its general outline, this is the Reformed or Calvinistic pattern for life in the world.

Reformed attitudes toward life in the world have had an immeasurably great effect on American history. Calvinistic convictions about living all of life for the glory of God led to the remarkable experiment of seventeenth-century New England, where Puritans created the freest, most stable, most democratic society then existing in the world. In the eighteenth century a more diffuse Puritan passion for public justice provided, if not the specific ideology, at least much of the energy for the American Revolution and the creation of a new nation. During the nineteenth century a more general evangelical Protestantism fueled immense labors of Christianization and civilization—subduing a continent, democratizing a people, evangelizing at home through revival and abroad through missions, reforming institutions, attitudes, habits, and social practices, and surviving a civil war that ended with the prohibition of slavery.

The encroachments of secularism on this Reformed deposit have changed the substance but not the form of public activity. When Science replaced Scripture, and Progress elbowed God aside, the goals remained the same—all of life must still be reformed. Only the agency was different. It might be Education, opened to all as a means for solving the nation's problems. It might be Science and Know-How, the Form and Demiurge of modernity. Most typically, the new religion has been government, or the state. With Democrats who favor social equality or Republicans who promote legislation for a free market, the crusading mentality remained. Thus, though modern Americans may differ in many particulars from their Puritan and evangelical ancestors, they still are deeply committed to working out their salvation, and the salvation of everyone else, through the re-structuring of public life.

THE ABSENCE OF "POLITICAL LUTHERANISM"

Conspicuously absent in American history has been the characteristi-cally Lutheran attitude. For one, it has been rare for Americans to think that a strategy for public life might look different from the axioms of private life. Instead, Puritan spirituality fueled the drive for a Puritan commonwealth. Evangelical revival became the model for evangelical social reform. The pragmatic approach to the self associated with John Dewey became a pragmatic method for regulating the public. The modern pursuit of absolute moral freedom became the drive for moral liberation in society. The notion that the public might operate under a different set of rules, that it might be possible to erect a theory of government transcending the values guiding the self, has been rare in American history.

Similarly, there has been only occasional recognition of what could be called "Lutheran irony." In religious terms, this irony is the sense that precisely when believers mount their most valiant public efforts *for* God, they run the greatest risk of substituting *their* righteousness for the righteousness of Christ, and thereby subverting justification by faith. A few Americans, like Nathaniel Hawthorne in the nineteenth century and Reinhold Niebuhr in the twentieth, may have glimpsed this irony, but it has been a distinctly minority position. In secular terms, "Lutheran irony" would be quick to perceive where the public crusade leads to unintended consequences: as constitutional changes to free the slaves lead to vastly expanded power for the courts, or efforts to make the world safe for democracy (Woodrow Wilson) lead to the rise of Hitler, or being willing to go anywhere in the defense of freedom (John F. Kennedy) leads to Vietnam, or a concern for national security (Richard Nixon) threatens the security of the nation's citizens (Watergate), or the desire for national defense heightens the risk of global annihilation. In situations both religious and secular, a "Lutheran" might be justified in asking if the direct transit from personal moral version to comprehensive public crusade did not lead to difficulties. If, in fact, there is a difference between God in relation to the individual and God in relation to the world, then a failure to observe the structural and systematic differences between personal moral vision and comprehensive public crusade becomes an important matter.

This book is not a condemnation of what I have called "Reformed" attitudes toward culture, nor is it primarily an effort to promote a "Lutheran" perspective. It is, rather, an effort to describe in general terms the nature of America's Christian heritage (which has been Reformed rather than Lutheran) and to show how that Reformed heritage has worked itself out through changing spheres in America's history. Were this book to be a comprehensive theoretical statement, it would require a lengthy totting up of strengths and weaknesses— Reformed strength in guiding the restructuring of societies, Reformed weakness in carrying reforming zeal to excess; Lutheran strength in recognizing the occasional incongruity between private and public spheres, Lutheran weakness in the tendency to lapse into political quietism. As it is, however, the book is concerned less with theory than with practice. America has in fact followed a Reformed pattern. What have been the results?

CHRISTIAN ALTERNATIVES: SEPARATISM

Before that examination begins, however, it is well to note two other characteristic attitudes toward life in the world that have arisen in Christian history but have been only marginally influential in America. A direct counterpoint to the Reformed pattern is offered by the separatist style, which, in Protestant history, was revitalized by the

Anabaptist movement of the sixteenth century. This Anabaptist approach to culture is the mirror image of the Calvinistic. At the time of the Reformation, Anabaptists were radical Protestants who felt that the corruption of both church and world required the formation of separated and purified communities. The Anabaptists rejected the baptism of infants because this rite, the basis for citizenship as well as an expression of faith, symbolized the mingled allegiance to church and world. Anabaptists also rejected military service because they felt that the coercion necessary to govern (or reform) an entire society was, in principle, contradictory to the ways of the Prince of Peace. Like the Reformed, Anabaptists sought a total renovation of the polity, but this renovation was to take place in alternative communities removed from the sinful world; they did not aim at subduing society as a whole for Christ.

From early in our settlement, America has been home to several varieties of Anabaptists, most notably the Mennonites and their extreme wing, the Amish. These *Stille im Lande* have sought salvation in separation from the world. They have concluded that since efforts to reform all of life and all of society are pretentious folly, true godliness must be cultivated in isolation from the sinful world.

American history has witnessed several variations on this theme. There was an Anabaptist leaven at Plymouth among the Pilgrims, at least with Governor William Bradford, who wondered late in his life if success in subduing the New World had not compromised the spirituality of the Pilgrims. During the nineteenth century, a parade of gifted, charismatic leaders abandoned efforts to reform all of society and instead went off into the wilderness to construct alternative communities where righteousness and truth could flourish at last. Transcendentalists at Brook Farm, the followers of John Humphrey Noyes at Oneida, and the Mormons under Joseph Smith and Brigham Young were among the best known who followed this path. In the twentieth century secular counterparts have arisen to this Anabaptist strategy, colonies of artists disgusted by the philistinism of the bourgeoisie or, more recently, communes of the disaffected who have tuned in, turned on, and dropped out.

In twentieth-century America, with its mass communication and its ever more tempting economic opportunities for any industrious group willing to enter the system, it has been very difficult for separatist bodies to maintain their distinct identity. To put it differently, the conditions of life in the recent history of the United States make it hard for visions of closed communities, like those of the Anabaptists, to survive in distinction from the mainstream society. The pattern that prevailed in early American history for the Quakers, come-outters who could never quite stay away, has been at work with Anabaptists and other sectarian bodies in this century. Mennonites, for example, have been too successful at exploiting the expansion of their educational opportunities, applying their work ethic in the modern economy, and even articulating a theoretical criticism of consumerism to preserve their separate identity. With some reluctance, they too have begun to enter the mainstream and form their opinions on public life in Reformed rather than Anabaptist terms. They too have begun to tell the rest of us what is good for us all.

If partially true for religious sectarians, then it is entirely true for their secular counterparts. The well-publicized leaders of countercultures from the 1960s never really escaped "the system." The tug of the mainstream—whether settled communities, settled families, settled incomes, settled employment—has been too strong. A countercultural note is still very strong *in* American public life, but it never really stood over against the larger culture. It too has become another secular variant of the Reformed desire to reshape public life according to the insights of a personal vision.

CHRISTIAN ALTERNATIVES: CATHOLIC SYNTHESIS

The history of Christianity reveals at least one other stance toward life in the world with some bearing on the American scene. In the Catholic Middle Ages, the institutions of religion and of government were integrated in ways combining some elements of both the later Reformed and Lutheran stances. With the later Lutherans, Catholics recognized that God exercised his sovereignty through different instrumentalities in the church and in the public sphere. With the Reformed, on the other hand, Catholics held that the spheres of church and society were of a piece. The church and the state were different, but were joined under a common divine sovereignty. Furthermore, Catholics held a belief that Protestants would later set aside, that God had established a hierarchy of rule in the church culminating in the papacy. This hierarchy not only directed the church but also provided the clearest model for social ordering of any kind. Ecclesiastical hierarchy thus become a model for political hierarchy. In addition, where institutions of public order and institutions of ecclesiastical order overlapped, it was only right for the public to defer to the church. H. Richard Niebuhr labeled this standpoint "Christ over culture."[7] In this description, it was a vision of life in which the church offers all other institutions a model of order to which they may aspire. In the centuries since the Reformation, European countries where Catholicism remained strong have adopted variations of this standpoint. Official recognition of the church, as well as governmental support for its particular offices, has been the norm. Yet in such circumstances the church has usually exercised its influence selectively, carefully watching the morality of its members and protecting its own interests against the state and other competing religions but otherwise keeping its distance from the exercise of governmental power.

Although the Roman Catholic church has been America's largest Christian denomination for over a century, American Catholics have rarely attempted to reproduce on these shores Continental attitudes toward culture. By the time Catholics arrived in force with the great nineteenth-century migrations, Protestant groups were too well established and the legal separation of church and state too deeply ingrained to permit even experimentation with the "Christ over culture" position in America. Throughout much of the nineteenth century, Roman Catholics more resembled the Anabaptists, building self-contained enclaves and a comprehensive network of institutions (schools, youth organizations, fraternal orders, insurance societies) as alternatives to the "public" (and largely Protestant) institutions of mainstream American culture. Soon, however, Catholics began to emerge from their immigrant ghettoes. When they did, however, they quickly assumed the Reformed attitude toward culture that was characteristic of their American neighbors. From the first major emergence of Catholics into the public life of America—which was probably the participation of several well-known bishops in temperance crusades during the late nineteenth century—Catholics in public have tended to act more like their Protestant fellow Americans than like their European fellow Catholics. Catholic efforts to professionalize higher education in the 1930s, to protect the nation from communists in the 1950s, and (through letters on nuclear arms and the economy from the bishops) to influence the direction of public policy in the 1980s have all reflected the Reformed spirit of American Christian politics.

In sum, the dominant religious outlook toward public life throughout American history has been Reformed, in either Christian or secular variations. Americans have committed themselves to ideals of the Good; they have then moved as if by second nature to formulating plans for letting all of society share that Good. They have mobilized followers for the effort of setting America, if not the whole world, to rights. The chapters that follow examine several episodes in which American Christians have followed this generally Reformed pattern, for good and for ill, in their efforts to shape the course of American public life.

II. HISTORY

3. The "Reformed" Politics of the American Revolution

The founding era of the United States offers a particularly fine historical laboratory for examining questions of religion and politics. Public spokesmen for Christianity played a significant role in promoting the movement for independence from Great Britain in the 1770s, and they rendered great service to the patriot cause during the Revolutionary War itself. In the years between the end of the conflict with Great Britain in the early 1780s and the reorganization of the United States government under the Constitution at the end of the decade, there was less public commentary by Christian leaders on political matters as such, yet believers regularly offered moral and religious contributions to the political process during that entire period. At every stage in that momentous era, American Christians were present, involved, and even in the forefront of promoting an independent United States of America.

The founding era is doubly important for our purposes since Christian political action appeared in different shapes during the period. In some particulars, to be sure, Christian action did remain constant, including both the practice of applying religious values to public life and the desire to align Christian teaching with the era's dominant political philosophy. Yet behavior immediately before and during the Revolutionary War was different in many important respects from behavior during the writing of the Constitution. To simplify a dynamically complex era, it may be said that during the Revolutionary period (that is, 1763–1783) Christian political involvement was direct, forceful, and unqualified, that it played a very important part in securing independence from Great Britain but that it also caused significant damage to the Christian faith and the integrity of the church. By contrast, Christian political involvement during the era of the Constitution (1783–1791) was more nuanced, restrained, and qualified; it played only a background role in the actual construction of the Constitution, but the results—for the nation and the church—were largely beneficial. The period as a whole illustrates how important an unrestrained "Reformed" approach to politics could be. During the Revolution, however, we see significant difficulties in that "Reformed" style. During the passage of the Constitution, when a leaven of restraint was added to "Reformed" politics, the results were much better.

Before and during the Revolutionary War, Christian faith played a political role at two levels. On the one hand, it contributed to the content of the period's dominant political ideology. In this regard, Christianity contributed its share to a powerful political ideology that, on balance, advanced the cause of justice. On the other hand, Christian faith was a significant force in the actual outworking of the war. In this regard, actions were less restrained, and results were not as good. Each of these deserves attention, but since the Revolutionary ideology was crucial throughout the entire period, including the era of the Constitution, we begin with it.

THE REPUBLICANISM OF THE FOUNDING ERA

Two crises dominated this era of American history. The first was a crisis of the British Empire and was resolved by the American Revolution. The second was a crisis of government in the new United States and was resolved by the delegates who convened in Philadelphia during the summer of 1787 to write the Constitution. In simplest terms, both represented an effort by Americans to preserve the virtues of *republican* government.

The War for Independence was fought because the American patriots thought the actions of Britain's Parliament were destroying traditional republican liberties. Americans who remained loyal to Britain shared many values with the patriots, but they felt that Parliament, though making mistakes in its treatment of the colonies, still provided better security for republican principles than the unknown, and seemingly anarchic, governments of the independent colonies.

Brief years after securing independence from Great Britain, worried leaders in several of the new states called for a Constitutional Convention because they feared that republicanism was threatened once again. This time, however, the threat came from within, especially from the undisciplined actions of the new state governments.

A HISTORY OF REPUBLICANISM

In eighteenth-century Britain and America, republicanism was an ideal rather than a sharply defined system. It arose with what could be called the political theorists of the Italian Renaissance, of whom Machiavelli is best known.[1] Republicanism took on a particular British cast during the English civil wars of the seventeenth century. While Oliver Cromwell and the armies of Parliament waged war against King Charles I for corrupting and oppressing the English people, theorists struggled to define the relationship between good government and social well-being. The range of thinkers who worried this subject was vast, including both the agnostic Thomas Hobbes and the Puritan John Milton. "Whig" thought, as republicanism was then often styled, also played a large role in England's Glorious Revolution of 1688, when Parliament removed King James II in favor of William and Mary of the Netherlands. In that crisis, as the leaders of 1688 saw it, the tyrannical aims of a Stuart monarch again imperiled the liberties of Englishmen. In this crisis leaders of the English Revolution replaced King James II not only because he acted capriciously as monarch but also because he embraced the Catholic faith, and so threatened the Protestant liberties won by the English Reformation. Besides replacing their king in 1688, leading "whigs" went further to compose a "Bill of Rights," which spelled out the irreducible liberties of at least the sort of English males who had led the Revolution, and also the concrete limits beyond which royal power could not go. In these efforts they were ably assisted by still more political theorists, of whom John Locke was most important.

Republican or "whig" ideas gradually receded in England over the course of the eighteenth century. Prime ministers like Horace Walpole and their parliaments still paid lip service to republican principles, but struggles for power at court as well as manuevering associated with England's expanding economy absorbed more energies than did efforts to define and extend republican liberties. An active coterie of thinkers outside of government felt very differently, however. These "true" or "real whigs" continued to write and agitate for an extension of republican ideals. Their voice did not make much of an impact in Britain, but it was heard clearly in America, where "real whig" principles throve. Eventually these principles became the basis for resistance to Great Britain and the construction of a new national government.

REPUBLICANISM DEFINED

What were republican principles? An additional question, with specific implications for Christian assessment, asks: What were the sources of these ideas?

Again in simplified terms, republicanism was the conviction that power defined the political process and that unchecked power led to corruption even as corruption fostered unchecked power. Furthermore, the arbitrary exercise of unchecked power must by its very nature result in the demise of liberty, law, and natural rights. "Real whigs," therefore, tended to favor separation of power in government rather than its concentration. They usually held that a good government must mix elements of popular influence, aristocratic tradition, and executive authority, rather than be simply democratic, simply aristocratic, or simply monarchical. Although most republicans early in the 1700s had their doubts about the wisdom of "the people," they held that governments must function for the common good (the "common weal" or "commonwealth") instead of for the promotion of private privilege or the advantage of a specific group. The very etymology of "republic," from *res publica* (the public thing), spoke to this concern. In addition, these "whigs" felt deeply that human beings possess a store of rights grounded in nature rather than the gift of a sovereign power (Locke defined these as "life, liberty, and [protection in the holding of] property"). Finally, republican theory drew a close connection between the morals of a people and the safety of its government—virtue in the public made it more likely that government would flourish, vice more likely that it would verge toward tyranny.

The key to republicanism was an effort to unite principles that had always been considered antithetical. Where security for private rights had been thought to require a strong monarch or aristocracy, republicans linked liberty and "popular government." Where the will of the people had been thought to lead inevitably to mob rule, republicans felt that a measure of popular participation could control the elites' abuse of power. Where virtue and power had once been considered separate themes, republicans bound them tightly together.

SOURCES OF REPUBLICANISM

Christians contributed their fair share to the formation of republicanism, though that process involved numerous individuals and groups over a long period of time. The Puritans who supported Cromwell or the Scottish Calvinists who agitated for the independence of their Presbyterian Kirk linked republican values with Scripture. They felt that republicanism represented a political recognition of the Bible's realistic teaching about human sinfulness and the ongoing struggle between Christ (who promoted true liberty) and Satan (who defined the worst possible tyranny). Other influences, however, were deistic or agnostic. Some of Britain's "real whigs" of the early eighteenth century had given up traditional Christian faith for a religion of nature with no place for miracles, the Incarnation, or special revelation.

Still other influences came from sources difficult to classify by religious conviction. Scottish and Irish nationalists supported republicanism because they detested the rule of England. Early modern scientists in the circle of Sir Isaac Newton were often whigs because they wanted to see the political order display the same harmony as the "laws" of nature revealed. Landowners whose property had been secured by the Glorious Revolution, lawyers who defended the prerogatives of the traditional common law, and philosophers who felt that the innate "moral sense" of human beings could dictate a just politics were only some of the others who promoted the development of republican ideals. In sum, the heritage of republicanism was mixed: it certainly had connections with biblical and Christian convictions, but also with many other sources.

REPUBLICANISM IN AMERICA

The exact shape of republican theory differed from place to place in Revolutionary America. In 1776, Thomas Jefferson could say that if the new Virginia state legislature passed four of the 126 bills proposed at its first session, the result would be "a system by which every fibre would be eradicated of antient or future aristocracy; and a foundation laid for a government truly republican." Jefferson's four essential bills repealed entail and primogeniture (ancient means of restricting ownership of land), prohibited taxes to support religion, and established a system of universal public education.[2] In Massachusetts, John Adams was more theoretical: The "true and only true definition of a republic" is "a government, in which all men, rich and poor, magistrates and subjects, officers and people, masters and servants, the first citizen and the last, are equally subject to the laws."[3]

Differ as they might over details, the patriots of the Revolution and the writers of the Constitution agreed on the need for republican government. The Declaration of Independence was a thesaurus of republicanism. It spoke much of "unalienable rights," it modified Locke to place "life, liberty, and the pursuit of happiness" among those rights, and it proclaimed the need for a "new government, laying its foundation on such principles, and organizing its powers in such form, as to . . . effect [the people's] safety and happiness." The Preamble of the Constitution, especially with its stated intention to "secure the blessings of liberty to ourselves and our posterity," likewise breathed the language of republicanism. Section 4 of Article IV explicitly guaranteed "to every State in this Union a republican form of government."

It was to preserve republican values that patriots fought the War for Independence. In 1766 Parliament had claimed "full power and authority to make laws . . . to bind the colonies and people of *America,* subjects of the crown of *Great Britain,* in all cases whatsoever."[4] The mother country showed its disregard for traditional liberties by taxing the colonists without their consent. Even if the taxes were small, the precedent was alarming. If Parliament could take away even a small portion of property simply because it wanted to, if the colonists had no power to check the exercise of parliamentary authority, then could not Parliament—as the Sons of Liberty proclaimed on every possible occasion in every possible way—take away all property, all religious freedom, all the traditional prerogatives of the colonies' governments, and even eventually human life itself? Both the question, and the background that gave it force, were thoroughly republican. In turn, the struggle for independence in America was a struggle for republicanism.

REPUBLICANISM AND THE CHRISTIAN FAITH

Republicanism was critical for the relation of religion and politics in the Revolutionary era, because the beliefs of American Christians paralleled republican principles in many particulars. This in turn led to the widespread assumption that republican principles expressed Christian values and that they could be defended with Christian fervor.

Republican political theory, particularly as it was expressed in the conflict with Great Britain, carried great intrinsic appeal for American Christians. Republicanism, no less than the Puritanism so important in American history, was a product of seventeenth-century English dissent. Together, the republican and the Puritan traditions shared many formal similarities.[5] In the first place, the Puritan and republican traditions both held, as one historian put it, "a distinctly bearish view of human nature."[6] Puritans dwelt at length on the natural tendency toward evil that arose as a consequence of Adam's fall. Republicans dwelt at length on the natural tendency to abuse official power as a consequence of the corrupting nature of power itself.

Puritans and republicans also defined virtue, freedom, and social well-being in very similar terms. Both saw virtue primarily as a negative quality: Puritans as the absence of sin, republicans as the absence of corrupt and arbitrary power. Puritans looked on freedom as liberation from sin, republicans as liberation from tyranny. The Puritans defined a good society as one in which sin was vanquished and in which people stood vigilantly on guard against its reappearance. Similarly, republicans defined a good society as one in which political freedom from tyranny was preserved and in which citizens resolutely resisted any tendency toward the corruption of power.

With their similar views on virtue, freedom, and social well-being, it is not surprising that republican and Christian points of view began to merge during the Revolution. It was only a small step, for example, to expand concern for the glorious liberty of the children of God into concern for the glorious freedoms imperiled by Parliament. This process was at work early on in the conflict with Great Britain and may be illustrated by a famous sermon that Jonathan Mayhew, a Boston Congregationalist, preached during the Stamp Act crisis of 1765. Parliament's tax on documents was odious to many colonists because it represented the attempt by an alien power to appropriate the property of Americans without their approval ("taxation without representation is tyranny"). At a time of great public agitation in Boston over the Stamp Act, Mayhew preached on Galatians 5:12–13 ("I would they were even cut off which trouble you. For brethren, ye have been called unto liberty; only use not liberty for an occasion to the flesh, but by love serve one another"). As Mayhew expounded this text, he seemed to say that the apostle had shown oppressed colonists how to resist the clutch of illegitimate parliamentary taxation.[7]

Republicans and the heirs of the Puritans also shared a common view of history. Both regarded the record of the past as a cosmic struggle between good and evil. To American Christians good and evil were represented by Christ and anti-Christ; to republicans, by liberty and tyranny. Both republicans and Puritans longed for a new age in which righteousness and freedom would flourish. Both hoped that the Revolution would play a role in bringing such a golden age to pass.

Republican and Christian points of view began to grow closer together after the French and Indian Wars (1756–1763) as Britain and the Church of England replaced France and Roman Catholicism as the great terrors in colonial eyes. For many American Christians, republican and Puritan perspectives soon became almost indistinguishable as the crisis with the British Parliament grew more intense. To many it soon seemed as if the two points of view shared common concerns, distrusted common foes, and defended common liberties. When, therefore, American Christians moved beyond thought to action, it was natural that republican principles shaped the nature of Christian response.

On balance, Christian faith offered an assist to republican theory. It kept republicanism alert to the dangers of runaway power, even as it restrained the utopian impulse to equate a republican society with a perfect society. Only when Christian values were merged into republican theory without remainder—when Christians began to speak of republicanism as an embodiment of Christianity itself—did serious difficulties arise.

CHRISTIAN POLITICAL ACTION IN THE REVOLUTION

During the actual conflict with Britain, Christian political action played a leading role in the achievement of independence. On the most general level, a broadly Puritan ethic set the tone for the patriots' political exertions. From the Puritan heritage, patriots found seriousness about the vocation of "public servant," an individual who sacrificed private gain for the public good. The same source provided an example of perseverance in the face of adversity—just as the earliest American settlers had continued to work hard and trust God when their enterprise was threatened by the forces of nature, so too could patriots labor on and pray when the tide of battle ran against them. Similarly, the Puritan link between personal virtue, the exercise of frugality, and the enjoyment of liberty served as a model for how the same qualities could be joined together in an independent United States.[8] On this level, Christian values shaped political behavior quite generally, but still with telling effect.

In other ways Christian political action was more direct. New England preachers had long stressed the special relationship between God and that region. As war approached many of them cast the conflict with Great Britain in cosmic terms. God had called his people to religious and political freedom in the New World; certainly he would now sustain them as they fought off the tyrannical effort by Parliament to destroy it.[9] New England was the scene of the sharpest early tensions with Britain; Boston patriots led in resisting parliamentary efforts to sustain a tax on tea (the Boston Tea Party), and the first actual battles of the war took place in Massachusetts (Lexington and Concord, Bunker Hill). It was thus of great significance for the whole American effort against Great Britain that a long New England tradition had recognized God as the Lord of Battles actively intervening on behalf of his people.

Sermons encouraging a defense of political liberty, however, were by no means restricted to New England. Presbyterians in New Jersey and the South preached a similar message, as did representatives of the Baptists and other smaller denominations. Even many clergymen of the Church of England, contradicting the official allegiance of their denomination, denounced the grasp of Parliament. To cite just one of hundreds of possible examples, a Virginian recorded the comments of his Anglican minister in 1774 after a sermon urging support for Boston after Parliament closed its port: "In the room of God save the king he cried out God Preserve all the Just rights and Liberties of America."[10]

The services of religion to the patriot cause were great and multiform. Ministers preached rousing sermons to militia bands as they met for training or embarked for the field. Many ministers served faithfully as chaplains. Ministers joined Christian laymen on the informal committees of correspondence that preceded the formation of the new state governments. Other ministers served gladly as traveling agents of the new governments, who wanted them to win over settlers in outlying areas to support the patriot cause. Throughout the conflict, common soldiers were urged to their duty by the repeated assertion that Britain was violating divine standards.[11]

Not all Christians in America supported the push toward independence so completely, or even supported it at all. A substantial number of Christians remained loyal to Great Britain. Throughout the colonies, especially in Pennsylvania, the population also included many Christian pacifists who felt both sides were wrong to fall to arms. And, as we shall see, there were also Christian patriots who made nice distinctions in what they did support and did not support in the war against the mother country.

THE "REFORMED" CONTRIBUTION OF CHRISTIANITY TO AMERICAN INDEPENDENCE

On the whole, however, the Christian faith was an important contributor to the patriot cause. Liberty was a supreme value in religious life, and so too it became supreme in political affairs. To preserve political liberty against the tyranny of Parliament was as intuitively the duty of Christians as to preserve spiritual freedom against the slavery of Satan. Christian support for the Revolution was, thus, "Reformed" as we defined the term earlier. Qualification, reserve, nuance, a recognition of ambiguity, or the effort to derive a well-orbed theory of political life were as out of place in defending colonial liberty against Parliament as they were in accepting the free offer of the gospel.

This direct political activity of Christians was of some consequence. Opponents recognized the importance of the Christian element immediately. A Hessian captain wrote of his experiences in Pennsylvania, "Call this war . . . by whatever name you may, only call it not an American Rebellion, it is nothing more or less than an Irish-Scotch Presbyterian Rebellion."[12] Joseph Galloway, a moderate opponent of Parliament who eventually chose loyalty to Great Britain over colonial independence, wrote that the colonial insurrection was led by "Congregationalists, Presbyterians, and Smugglers."[13] From the patriot side the connotations were different, but the message was largely the same.

A modern historian, Patricia Bonomi, concluded a lengthy examination of religion's role in the Revolution with a fuller judgment, but one that makes substantially the same point:

> Religious doctrine and rhetoric, then, contributed in a fundamental way to the coming of the American Revolution and to its final success. In an age of political moderation, when many colonials hesitated at the brink of civil war, patriotic clergymen told their congregations that failure to oppose British tyranny would be an offense in the sight of Heaven. Where political theory advised caution, religious doctrine demanded action. By turning colonial resistance into a righteous cause, and by crying the message to all ranks in all parts of the colonies, ministers did the work of secular radicalism and did it better: they resolved doubts, overcame inertia, fired the heart, and exalted the soul.[14]

PROBLEMS WITH REVOLUTIONARY CHRISTIANITY

The problem with Christian political action in the Revolutionary period was not necessarily the link with republican theory, nor necessarily the support of independence. It is possible to question whether colonial believers should have joined their faith so securely to republican principles, or whether the Revolutionary conflict qualified as a "just war" in classical Christian definition. But these matters are not the most obvious difficulties in the Christian support of the Revolution. The problem has as much to do with political style as political content. It was the unreserved embrace of the cause, the all-or-nothing identification of the patriot position as *the* Christian position, that strikes the modern observer most forcefully. The problem at this point is not political so much as it is religious. It concerns the effect of such political action on the content of the faith.

Some observers at the time saw the difficulty. Ezra Stiles, a minister in Newport, Rhode Island, who later became president of Yale College, had been repulsed by the theological and social turmoil of the Great Awakening, the series of religious revivals during the 1740s that exerted an especially strong effect in New England. As he saw the Awakening, it had been a time when wrangling of all sorts—theological, ecclesiastical, political, and economic—had obscured the central message of Christianity. As tensions with Britain rose in the 1760s and 1770s, Stiles felt the same uneasiness as he had during the revival. If the gospel had suffered when all New England was convulsed by disagreement over a religious event, how much more would it suffer when a political controversy rolled over the region. Stiles himself was an ardent, even an ecstatic, defender of colonial liberties and supporter of the move toward independence, but he also resolved that political topics would not intrude into his sermons and that his status as a servant of Christ should keep him circumspect in political action. As he put the matter in 1772, "I am a Friend to American Liberty. . . . [But] We [ministers] have another Department, being called to an Office and Work, which may be successfully pursued . . . under every species of *Civil Tyranny* or *Liberty*. We cannot become the Dupes of Politicians without Alliances, Concessions and Connexions dangerous to evangelical Truth and spiritual Liberty."[15]

Stiles, however, was in a minority. Much more typical in fact were "Alliances, Concessions and Connexions" that worked at direct cross purposes with "evangelical Truth." The most obvious example of political allegiance dictating religious understanding was the use of the Bible. During the period of heightened tensions, it proved nearly impossible to preserve the Scriptures as an independent spiritual authority. The temptation to employ the Bible for partisan purposes was nearly irresistible. In the momentous year of 1776, for example, two different clergymen preached on Revelation 13 and identified the Beast described in that passage as British tyranny.[16] One of these was Samuel Sherwood of Weston, Connecticut, who described British oppression of the colonies as the Antichrist. John's seven-headed Beast, according to Sherwood, was nothing other than "the corrupt system of tyranny and oppression, that had been fabricated and adopted by the ministry and parliament of Great Britain."[17]

Even before 1776 it had become common to line up the American defense of liberty with positive stories, images, and injunctions from the Bible—Joseph, Moses, the Exodus, "the liberty wherewith Christ had made us free"—and to align America's foes with the negative— Pharaoh, Egypt, Babylon, spiritual tyranny. The practice had existed even before American-British relations turned sour. As early as 1756, for example, in the early days of the French and Indian War, a Presbyterian evangelist from Virginia, Samuel Davies, spoke of the conflict between the Protestant British empire and the Catholic French empire as "the commencement of this grand decisive conflict between the Lamb and the beast." The defeat of the French, Davies held, would produce nothing less than "a new heaven and a new earth."[18]

As the war with France faded into the background, it became obvious that a miscalculation had occurred. It was not so much Roman Catholic French tyranny that was the Antichrist as it was tyranny itself. And so when Parliament, King George III, and Britain's colonial ministry acted (as it seemed) tyrannically toward the colonies, it was a small matter to employ the Bible's terminology as the language of this new conflict.

The Revolutionary crisis also led to a disturbing tendency to employ theological language in the service of the patriot cause. During the Stamp Act crisis of 1765, for example, defenders of the colonies hailed each other as the "darlings of Providence" and "the Lord's anointed."[19] After the port of Boston was closed by Parliament's Coercive Acts in 1774, the pastors of Connecticut wrote to their Boston colleagues, praying particularly that in the present crisis God would "ensure Salvation to us."[20] To Abraham Keteltas of Newburyport, Massachusetts, the struggle with Britain was not primarily a constitutional one; it was rather "the cause of truth against error and falsehood . . . the cause of heaven against hell."[21] More directly, the Presbyterian Robert Smith enunciated explicitly what others had only assumed implicitly when he declared in 1781 that "the cause of America is the cause of Christ."[22] Some of these expressions were self-conscious metaphors. Others seem to have been taken literally. If they were intended as literal statements of fact, it was no longer the Scripture that illuminated the condition of the colonists, but the conditions of patriotism that showed what the Bible meant.

The political allegiances of the period also led to the needless disruption of ecclesiastical fellowship. Because Eli Forbes, the Congregational minister of Brookfield, Massachusetts, believed that Christians should not engage in needless warfare against each other, he and his wife were stoned by erstwhile members of his congregation and he was driven entirely from the ministry.[23] Because the Presbyterian Synod of North Carolina wavered in declaring for the patriot cause, the powerful Synod of New York and Philadelphia threatened to break off ecclesiastical fellowship.[24] In these and many other similar incidents, the patriot Christians left no doubt as to their ultimate loyalties.

THE POLITICAL SUBVERSION OF CHRISTIANITY

The problem with this sort of Christian political behavior is its subversion of Christianity. The Christian message is a universal one that, as Ezra Stiles saw clearly, "may be successfully pursued . . . under every species of *Civil Tyranny* or *Liberty.*" The problem was not first of all the patriots' political principles. A decent case can in fact be made that the freedom to work out the implications of Christianity in a modern Western culture leads naturally to something like the republicanism of the Revolutionary period. Nor was the problem political participation itself. Rather, it was the style of political participation, the mode of political behavior. Patriot Christians moved without hesitation from the observation that some actions of Parliament compromised colonial rights to the conclusion that Parliament was promoting tyranny and that this promotion of tyranny was the Antichrist.

Given that leap, it was only appropriate to treat the war with Britain as a climactic struggle between good and evil.

Christian support of the American Revolution is thus an extreme case illustrating the kind of culture-shaping efforts that had characterized the "Reformed" wing of Protestantism since the Reformation. During the Revolution, weaknesses in that approach were exacerbated. Patriots did not take time to construct theoretical principles for Christian political activity, so their actions were precipitous and driven by emotion. They did not feel compelled to look for the ambiguities in the actions of Parliament or in their own reactions, so they fell into black-and-white habits of mind in which the patriots could do no wrong and Britain no right. They thoroughly identified the cause of America with the cause of Christ, so they lost the ability to apply the Christian message across the board. As intense as they were in defending the righteousness of the patriot cause, they could not hear the gospel's message of forgiveness for their foes or its call to repentance for themselves. The translation of a personal vision of righteousness under God to public policy embodying that vision was a major force in securing the success of the Revolution. The very factors that made this process so influential, however, were the same factors that made it a disaster for the integrity of the Christian faith itself.

A DISCRIMINATING PATRIOTISM

The record of Christian patriotism during the Revolution does contain its better moments. Some Christians who favored the cause against Parliament did in fact make the critical distinctions that were so often absent among fellow Christians and patriots. One of the brightest examples of such discriminating political action was provided by the Reverend Samuel Hopkins, who was, like Ezra Stiles, a Congregational minister in Newport, Rhode Island. Hopkins's politics shared much with his contemporaries. He opposed the actions of Parliament as illegitimate assaults on the colonists' traditional liberties, and he fully supported independence once negotiations with Parliament broke down. What distinguished Hopkins from his fellows was possession of an overarching theology of social action and an ability to apply that theory with discrimination to the lived realities of his own situation.

Hopkins was a student of Jonathan Edwards, the leader of the Great Awakening and also the leading theologian of the American colonial period. From Edwards, Hopkins took a principle of theological ethics that became his guide for behavior in the public sphere. Edwards had defined true virtue as "love to Being in general," by which he meant that men and women were to order their actions toward any particular object in accordance with that object's true worth.[25] God, as perfect Being, deserved perfect love and obedience. The church, as the bride of Christ, deserved respect as a high and holy entity. Human beings, as those who bore God's image, deserved to be treated with full respect.

In addition, Edwards had also impressed upon Hopkins the need to restrict the visible church to individuals who had made a specific profession of faith in Christ. In this Edwards was reacting to customary practices in New England whereby church membership was granted to all who lived respectable lives and professed a general belief in the Christian religion. For Edwards, the division between church and world was sharper than that. He convinced Hopkins and a considerable group of Hopkins's contemporaries that the "being" of the church required it to be separated somewhat more distinctly from the world.

When the Revolution approached, Hopkins took an interest in political matters, even to the point of arguing in private for the patriot cause. But Hopkins's patriotism was different from that of others who merged their Christianity and their politics. His carefully constructed ethical position and his Edwardsean view of the church gave him an unusual perspective on Revolutionary events. Though he was a patriot, he was self-consciously first a Christian. As such, he was able to separate political and Christian allegiances. And because he did not simply define his Christianity in terms of patriotic needs, he was also able to bring a specifically Christian critique to bear on *American* society.

Hopkins's particular social concern about America during the Revolution was the preservation of slavery. In a pamphlet sent to members of the Continental Congress in 1776, Hopkins asked pointedly how the colonies could complain about "enslavement" by Parliament when they practiced a much worse form of slavery themselves. He asked the representatives to "behold the *sons of liberty,* oppressing and tyrannizing over many thousands of poor blacks, who have as good a claim to liberty as themselves."[26] Hopkins wondered if slaves were not also humans made in the image of God? Did not the slave trade wantonly violate the prohibition of the sixth commandment against stealing? And, most importantly, did not the practice of slavery make it much more difficult to communicate the gospel to the slaves?

A few others joined Hopkins in such discriminating political action during the Revolution, but not many. It was not mere happenstance that Hopkins and most of those who shared his position were followers of Jonathan Edwards. As heirs of the colonial Awakening, they had made a sharp mental distinction between the church and the world. They were less prone than their fellows simply to equate the cause of Christianity and the general benefit of the colonies. In addition, the ethical theory that he had derived from Edwards's concept of virtue provided an independent base for assessing political developments. Hopkins and like-minded followers of Edwards were not, that is, exclusively dependent upon republican theory. Their own theology acted as a leaven or balance to the principles of republicanism. Hopkins himself saw little conflict between Edwards ethics and the principles of republicanism, but the fact that he was conscious of bringing *both* of them to bear on the Revolutionary situation meant he had a better chance of preserving some integrity for a distinctly Christian vision in the crucible of the Revolution.

WEIGHING THE BALANCE

The story of Christian political involvement in the American Revolution is a sobering one. The Christian contribution to republican theory was substantial, as was direct support in the battle for independence. Without the aid of the churches it would certainly have proven more difficult to separate the colonies from the mother country. To the extent, therefore, that the Revolution represented the justifiable defense of traditional liberties, the Christian convictions of American citizens must be given some of the credit for the establishment of the United States.

At the same time, ardent Christian support of the war effort led also to the compromising of the Christian faith itself. The righteousness of the American cause loomed as "another god" in competition with the God of traditional Christianity. Wholehearted Christian support of the patriot effort ended by undercutting Christianity. Only with occasional spokesmen like Samuel Hopkins did Christianity act as an independent force in the period. More generally, the absence of theoretical guidelines for the application of Christian values in the political process and a failure to discriminate between secondary political values and primary religious principles compromised the very faith that was being directed to serve the patriot cause.

Christian political behavior during the Revolution drew on the two great religious strands of the colonial period, Puritanism and the Great Awakening. Like earlier Puritans, patriots of the Revolutionary era were deeply concerned about the moral dimensions of politics and society. They knew as instinctively as their Puritan ancestors did that the realm of politics was a moral one in which the standards of Christianity were as viable as they were in personal and church life. And so, like the Puritans before them, the patriots approached the political decisions of their day as Christian questions needing to be addressed in Christian terms. The specific Calvinistic theology of the Puritans had given way to a more general Protestant faith—or with some important leaders, to a vague deism—but the moral approach to public life remained the same.

The patriots also embodied patterns of religious life from the colonial revival, the Great Awakening. Just as in the revival, fervent rhetoric was appropriate to describe the decision for spiritual life or death, so in "the crisis, the period that tried men's souls"—to quote Tom Paine—fervent rhetoric was appropriate to describe the choice for liberty or tyranny. Over the passage of three decades, the style of the revival became the style for political mobilization.[27] The appeal to choose life broadened out as years went by from the spiritual to the political. Where once revivalists had gathered crowds by describing the battle of Christ and Satan, patriots with revivalistic rhetoric inspired the masses to join the struggle against tyranny. The content was different, but the form remained the same.

If my judgments are correct, that is not, however, the end of the story. The matter is more complicated because of the conjunction of two realities. First, if the actions of America's Christian patriots were important in the Revolutionary period, it was because they embodied the form and spirit of previous religious movements. The Revolution was neither a Puritan movement nor a revival, but its religious coloration is unthinkable without the precedents of Puritanism and the Great Awakening. Second, if American Christian acted irresponsibly with respect to Christianity itself during the Revolutionary period, their very irresponsibility also contributed to their influence. Judicious, even-handed Christian support did not make much of an impression. Samuel Hopkins may have made wise discriminations, but colonists heeded much more the voices of ministers who urged wholehearted commitment to the cause of independence.

All this seems to lead to a troubling conclusion. The events of the Revolution might lead us to think that if Christians want to influence public policy, they should apply their Christian faith as recklessly and as unreservedly as possible, even at the risk of the faith itself. To introduce nuance, discrimination, or theory would seem to lessen the likelihood of success. However, the period immediately after the Revolution suggests that these may not be the only options. Under another set of circumstances, there may be a better way.

4. A Better Way: Theory, Compromise, and the Constitution

The winning of independence from Great Britain and the writing of the United States Constitution were obviously different events. The first was public to the widest extent possible; it featured a lengthy war, and it led to the establishment of a new nation. By contrast, although concern for the nature of government in the new United States was widespread, the Constitution was written in private by a group of only fifty-five men. The lapse of years from the first efforts to reform the Articles of Confederation in the mid-1780s to the passage of the Bill of Rights in 1791 was considerable, but these public discussions did not dominate public attention as had the War for Independence. And although the Constitution represented a new framework of government, it was as much an extension of principles in the Declaration of Independence and the Articles of Confederation as an expression of something entirely new. All this is to say that to compare Christian political action in the Revolutionary War to Christian political action in the writing of the Constitution is to compare two different things. No direct parallels or simple contrasts should be expected.

The nature of Christian involvement in these two events is so strikingly different as to be noteworthy. Intense, even fervent involvement in the first gave way to much more casual concern about the second. A concentrated effort to depict the war in directly biblical terms gave way to a relative absence of preaching on the constitutional crisis. Issues of religion and politics, especially concerning the relation between the institutions of church and state, did concern many Christians at the time of the writing of the Constitution, but the level of religious rhetoric remained lower during the latter period than it was in the former.

If these generalizations are correct, however, we are left with an odd situation. As I argued in the last chapter, direct Christian involvement played a large role in the Revolution, but the result was not particularly favorable for the Christian message itself. On the other hand, Christian involvement was much reduced during the writing of the Constitution, but, I shall contend in this chapter, the result was much more favorable for Christianity. Therein lies a tale that suggests something more general about fruitful Christian involvement in the political process. But first it is necessary to outline the events that brought Americans from the triumph of the Revolution to the crisis of the Constitution.

FROM THE REVOLUTION TO THE CONSTITUTION

The story of the Constitution, like the story of the Revolution, concerns the use of republican ideas to meet the political needs of the hour. But though the ideas remained roughly the same, the circumstances had changed dramatically. The period from the end of the Revolutionary War to the ratification of the Constitution is not as well known as that of the war itself, but it reflects no less the power of republicanism.[1] The Articles of Confederation, which were to rule the newly independent United States, went into effect in 1781. Very soon thereafter leaders throughout the country began to ask if this instrument of government was doing the job. The Articles established a national legislature very much dependent upon the goodwill and financial contributions of the states for their authority. Under the Articles, the country possessed a weak, rotating executive (little more than a chairman). Each state, from populous Virginia, Pennsylvania, and Massachusetts to tiny Rhode Island and Delaware, had an equal vote in all deliberations. The Congress of Confederation had no authority to raise money on its own initiative but was required to request funds from the states. And the Articles could be amended only by the unanimous consent of all thirteen states.

A few recent historians have argued that things were not as difficult under the Articles as their detractors supposed. But whatever the actual state of affairs, influential spokesmen in many of the states began to worry. Their perception has shaped the traditional and majority opinion of historians that from 1781 to 1787 in the United States was a "critical period."

PROBLEMS OF THE ARTICLES: ECONOMIC AND POLITICAL

Problems under the Articles were manifold, including economic uncertainties that undercut the ability of the nation to conduct its foreign affairs. Chief among these was the issue of "funding" the war debt. Who should repay the loans taken out by the Continental Congress from France and other foreign powers to pay for the fight against Britain? As it turned out, the war debt was passed to the states. Some payed on it conscientiously, some did not. Without a secure, reliable system of repayment, the United States had little faith and credit among other nations. In addition, when the war debt reverted to the states, it meant that the debt was no longer useful as a national currency. Alexander Hamilton of New York, who was especially concerned about the promotion of trade and industry in the new country, considered it a disaster for states to control instruments of debt, since this restricted the circulation of credit within the new nation.

Other economic problems also bedeviled the new country. Some of the states issued vast quantities of paper money. This fueled extreme inflation, which in turn threatened to upset all economic planning and to undercut habits of frugality, thrift, and fiscal discipline among the population. Under the Articles, the national government was powerless to do anything about it.

The government also seemed powerless to remedy its own defects. The necessity for unanimity among the states to amend the Articles led to a series of defeats for national measures. The last straw for those dissatisfied with the Articles came in 1786 when a majority, but not all, of the states agreed to give the Congress power to tax imports as a way of providing a source for its own funds. Without a unanimous vote to change its way of raising money, Congress continued to function with very little actual authority.

PROBLEMS OF THE ARTICLES: MORAL

Economic and political problems, in sum, loomed large under the Articles, but they did not seem as important as moral concerns to James Madison and several of the other figures who would take the lead in writing a new constitution. Madison, who had already served in the Virginia legislature as well as in the national congress, was especially upset at the way in which government under the Articles seemed to be violating the principles of republicanism. The United States had fought a bloody war with Great Britain to ensure the perpetuation of republican ideals, but no sooner was this war over than Americans seemed to turn their backs on these principles.

The growth of factionalism was one sign of dangerous corruption. Madison and like-minded observers were appalled at the division in some states between a debtor class advocating "easy money" and a creditor class demanding a stable currency. They were particularly dismayed at the short-lived, but troubling, "rebellion" of Daniel Shays in western Massachusetts. Massachusetts possessed one of the most admired state constitutions, and it had run its financial affairs with considerable care. Yet in 1786 hard-pressed debtor farmers in the western part of the state revolted under Shays, a former captain in the militia, to prevent foreclosures and procure debtor relief. The prospect of economic conflict and social anarchy badly frightened those who felt that the promise of America was not being fulfilled.

For Madison, however, the greatest moral difficulty was not the chaos threatened by the likes of Daniel Shays. The really troubling development was the decline of republican practice in the state governments. Reacting against the arbitrary exercise of power by British judicial and executive actions, the new state constitutions vested vast powers in popularly elected legislatures. As the states carried out their governmental responsibilities, two difficulties emerged. The state legislatures tended to be large, which meant that the districts of representatives were small. Madison thought he perceived a disturbing trend in those small districts. Rather than electing men of gravity and substance to conduct the affairs of the states, voters were turning to men of little consequence or even to rabble-rousers and demagogues.

As if this were not bad enough, the legislatures conducted by such individuals often acted with extraordinary disregard for checks and balances on power. Madison and his friends made diligent efforts to collect the news from other states, and what they discovered was not encouraging. During the 1780s, to use but one example, the New Hampshire legislature repeatedly vacated or suspended the judgments of judges, arbitrarily examined appeals and initiated cases in law, and in general arrogated to itself many traditionally executive and judicial functions.[2]

TOWARD PHILADELPHIA

The question Madison, Alexander Hamilton, John Adams, and other veterans of the Revolutionary struggle asked themselves was a grave one. Had the war to preserve republicanism against Britain succeeded, only to witness the decline of republicanism in an independent America? Were European skeptics in fact correct that it was foolish to think that people could govern themselves with justice in such a large place as the United States?

This was the situation and these were the fears that lay behind the call for the 1787 Convention in Philadelphia to remedy the defects of the Articles. As proponents of a stronger national government interpreted the events of their own time, the Convention seemed to represent a last chance for bringing together "popular government" and "individual freedom," for securing the goals toward which republican ideals pointed.

Although this situation posed a crisis nearly as grave as the crisis of independence, it generated far less explicitly Christian comment than had the war with Britain. After their intense involvement with politics in the 1770s, America's Christian leaders had largely turned aside from the political arena. Many of them continued to be concerned about the well-being of society and to speak out on matters of public morality, yet politics was no longer the key. A recent historian has summarized the concerns of religious leaders in the 1780s with the following apt description:

In the postwar period, after American independence had been successfully won and attention turned increasingly to internal problems, it became clear that the establishment of republican government was not itself a sufficient basis for American happiness. Only through education, the cultivation of private and public morality, and—the clergy in particular insisted—the regeneration of Christian faith, would the American republic realize its exalted millennial goal.[3]

The one exception to this political passivity was the church-state question as debated in several of the states as they prepared their new constitutions. In Virginia, Massachusetts, South Carolina, and elsewhere, there was considerable discussion of how the state governments could promote the virtue among the citizens necessary for the survival of republican governments. Many leaders in the new states felt that religion was important for this cause, yet they were reluctant, as republicans, to give government the kind of power in religion that England had exercised through the Anglican church. Although Virginia followed out the logic of the Revolution and completely removed government from any official influence on religious life, most of the other states came up with compromises. The new constitutions in Massachusetts and South Carolina, for example, both guaranteed complete freedom of religion to its citizens. But then Massachusetts proceeded to give the legislature power to promote public worship and religious training, a power it exercised by granting certain favors and exemptions to the Congregational church. (Massachusetts's mild establishment of Congregationalism, which always included toleration for other denominations, was not repealed until 1833.) South Carolina granted no particular favors to any one denomination but did decree that the "Christian Protestant religion" was "the established religion of the state."[4]

In general, however, Christians took little religious interest in the larger constitutional questions of the 1780s. Only a few special sermons were preached at the time of the Constitutional Convention, and only marginal religious concern attended the delegates as they made their way to Philadelphia in the summer of 1787.

A NEW, REPUBLICAN CONSTITUTION

In the event, the Convention did bend to the will of the nationalists like Madison, Hamilton, Adams, and also George Washington, Thomas Jefferson, Benjamin Franklin, and the other well-known founders.[5] Still, these proponents of a strong national government did not obtain all they had wanted. Madison, for example, hoped that under the new Constitution the president and the Supreme Court would be given the power to veto legislative acts of the state governments. He also felt that in order to avoid abuses of power by the state governments, both houses of the national legislature should be apportioned according to the size of the states.

But the founders accomplished their most important goals. They succeeded in strengthening both the power of popular sovereignty and the power of the nation. With a few strategic compromises, they were able to win over many of the staunchest defenders of the states' rights. The preservation of apportionment by state unit in the Senate and the important role given to the states in the electoral college reassured those defenders that the national government would not be too strong.

The central thrust of the Constitution lay in its balance of powers, a balance of powers that would, in theory, prevent any segment of the national government from becoming too powerful, while also allowing that national government to check the arbitrary exercise of government in the states. So on the national level, the powers of the legislature, the president, and the courts were spelled out in such a way that each exercised some kind of restraint on the other two. The president, for example, could veto legislation from Congress, but Congress could override the veto if it secured larger majorities. The president was commander in chief of the military, but only Congress could declare war. The president appointed justices of the Supreme Court, but the Senate confirmed those appointments. On the other hand, the delegates at Philadelphia seemed simply to assume that the Supreme Court could rule on the constitutionality of laws from the federal legislature, although this power was not mentioned directly in Article III, which established the national judiciary. The new Constitution also gave the

Congress power to levy excise taxes and taxes on imports, but it withheld the power to tax the property of individual citizens directly. (Only in 1913 did the Sixteenth Amendment provide for a direct tax on personal income.)

The Constitution also succeeded in addressing the issues that had particularly troubled James Madison. The people at large were provided a significant voice in protecting their own liberties, directly through the election of representatives to the House and indirectly in the choice of state legislatures who, in turn, selected United States senators and determined the way electors for presidents were chosen. (The direct power of the people was increased when the states provided for the popular election of presidential electors and when, in 1913, the Seventeenth Amendment established the direct popular election of senators.) In addition, the first ten amendments to the Constitution (The Bill of Rights) were passed immediately after the formation of the new government, and these contained many provisions guaranteeing the liberties of individual citizens.

At the same time, the new Constitution provided for only two senators and a small number of representatives from each state (Virginia was given the most, with ten; Rhode Island and Delaware received one each). These provisions were thought to increase the chance that men of distinction, known widely for their wisdom and gravity, would be selected by the people at large for the House and by the state legislatures for the Senate. In turn, the various levels of state and national government provided many checks against the threat of democratic mob rule. Where the will of the people played a very large role in government, the Constitution also sought to protect the rights of minorities and to make it difficult to bring about fundamental alterations in the government.

Finally, the Constitution was also balanced by a retention of a fair measure of state power. The state governments did indeed lose considerable authority under the Constitution, but they retained a full measure of control over their own internal affairs. The Fourteenth Amendment, passed after the Civil War, included the provision that "no state shall make or enforce any law which shall abridge the privileges or immunities of citizens of the United States." This tended to increase the power of the national government over the states and their citizens, but that amendment did not entirely override the Tenth Amendment in the Bill of Rights from 1791, which decreed that "powers not delegated to the United States by the Constitution, nor prohibited by it to the States, are reserved to the States respectively, or to the people."

In the context of its time, the central argument of those who favored the new Constitution was that republicanism could work, and indeed worked best, in a nation like the new United States. James Madison with Alexander Hamilton and John Jay wrote a series of eighty-five *Federalist Papers* to promote the approval of the Constitution in the state ratifying conventions. The most famous of these essays was Madison's *Tenth Federalist,* which made the case that republicanism required a large and diverse country. Europe's experiments at republican government had failed largely because they had been attempted in tiny places where the popular will could be manipulated by local potentates. In America it was different. Madison admitted that both the democratic provisions of the Constitution and the powerful national offices it provided could be abused. People by nature were power-hungry, and human nature would not change under the Constitution. Yet because the United States was so large, because it included so many diverse interests (economically, religiously, politically), the republican balance of powers had a better chance to work here than anywhere else. Selfish interests (state versus state, state versus nation, class versus class, section versus section) would cancel each other out. And with dignified elected representatives who were concerned about the common good, there was an even greater chance that the corruptions of power and the efforts to gain and manipulate power could be overcome.

The Constitution, in sum, rested on a realistic view of people but an optimistic view of republicanism. If government could be structured in such a way as to ensure that the better sort of people were selected to rule by democratic means, and if government could be built to prevent excessive concentration of power in any one sector, then the state might both protect the liberties of the people and still exercise sufficient power to set firm national policy and flourish in the world at large.

For our purposes, the two key features of the Constitution-writing process were its reliance on republican theory and the willingness of its authors to compromise in pursuit of its passage. In the first instance, the founders' work rested in part on their growing opposition to intuitive politics; that is, they had come to question the wisdom of America's early state governments, which established policies simply by reflex in reaction to the abuses of British rule. If Parliament's ministers had been too powerful, then the executives of the new state governments must be rendered powerless. If the colonies had suffered from a lack of representatives in Parliament, then the new states must provide large legislatures with many representatives. If the will of the people had been scorned under the old regime, then the new governments must exalt democracy above all else. The authors of the Constitution questioned this style of politics by reaction. They did not minimize the abuses under British rule, but they also recognized abuses in the reactions against them. Their solution was to spend more time working out a *theory of government* that could guide political action. It should not be thought that the republican theory of James Madison, or the somewhat different theory of Alexander Hamilton, were necessarily perfect. Nonetheless, they did show how valuable it was to spend time and energy formulating a general conception of government and its duties before attempting to promote political action. Theirs was a cohesive *theory,* and action guided by it represented a significant advance over that of the Revolutionary period, when American government was more a product of reaction to abuses than an expression of positive principles.

In the second instance, the Constitution would never have come into existence if its strongest supporters had not been willing to compromise with opponents in securing its passage. The negotiation that led to the plan of apportionment for the House and Senate (the House by population, the Senate with equality for the states) was only the most famous of the many compromises that were necessary. Had proponents of a new government been unyielding in their drive for a stronger national power, there would have been no Constitution. But within the boundaries set by their most general concerns, the founders were quite flexible.

The founders' reliance on republican theory and their willingness to compromise in pursuit of their political goals are central features of their work. These themes also provide a bridge to a more direct consideration of the fate of Christianity in the Constitutional era.

THE CONSEQUENCES OF THE CONSTITUTION FOR CHRISTIANITY

Any effort to judge the consequences of the Constitution for Christianity must take into account two things: the major goals of the founders and the relation of these goals to Christian principles and activities.

As we have seen, the founders' first goal was to secure a republican government. Second, they sought to strengthen the character of America's citizens as the central prop for upholding the Constitution itself. They presupposed that a direct and intimate bond linked the success of any government and the general values, or morals, of its people. This was especially true for republican government. If a government "of the people" was to secure peace and prosperity, it must rest on a citizenry of wisdom and virtue. Many of the schemes for promoting widespread education in the early years of the United States stated this matter directly. The Massachusetts Constitution of 1780, echoing the sentiments of John Adams, Thomas Jefferson, James Madison, and other national leaders, spelled it out directly: "Wisdom and knowledge, as well as virtue, diffused generally among the body of the people [is] necessary for the preservation of their rights and liberties."[6]

On this matter Christians in the new republic could not have been more thoroughly in agreement. They too felt that the health of the new nation depended ultimately on the character of the citizenry. As a New Jersey minister, John Woodhull, put it on November 26, 1789, in a sermon celebrating the establishment of the new Constitution: "God usually, and I believe always, treats nations, considered as publick bodies, according to their general moral character."[7] Woodhull's final advice to his congregation, therefore, was to pursue morality in private life as the best way of assuring greatness for the nation. Political and religious leaders in the new United States agreed that governments succeeded or failed according to the character of their citizens. The practical question that remained was how to promote that necessary

THE CONSTITUTION / 65

goodness. The answer of the founders brings us to a third major purpose of the men who wrote the Constitution.

SEPARATION OF CHURCH AND STATE

The founders thought a strict separation between the institutions of the church and the institutions of the national government essential for the general health of the commonwealth and the specific promotion of virtue in the population. Sixteen simple words in the First Amendment of 1791 made the point unambiguously: "Congress shall make no law respecting an establishment of religion, or prohibiting the free exercise thereof." How the founders' desire is to be interpreted at the end of the twentieth century is a matter for contention. What it meant in 1787 is quite clear. The founders held that the establishment of religion—official governmental support and funding for one form of Christianity—had been a blight in Europe. The establishment of religion had led to oppression and the denial of liberties that were part of natural rights. State-supported bishops, ecclesiastical courts, and religious tests for public office had all subverted the rights of life, liberty, property, and the pursuit of happiness.

The convictions that found expression in the First Amendment rested on several more general principles. Most of the men who wrote the Constitution welcomed the influence of religion on public life, but they wanted that influence to remain implicit, to be an indirect force in guiding public policy rather than an institutionalized agency participating directly in public affairs. Religion was to be a context for political behavior (many would have said the necessary context), not a concern of the political process itself.

The history leading to the First Amendment and the division between the institutions of state and church was a long one in America. Significantly, it included a strong tradition that opposed religious establishment for Christian rather than political reasons. Roger Williams was expelled from Massachusetts in the 1630s and forced to settle in Rhode Island in part because he argued that churches were corrupted by power when they allied themselves with the state. As he put it in his famous tract on *The Bloody Tenet of Persecution for Cause of Conscience:* "God requireth not an uniformity of religion to be enacted and enforced in any civil state; which enforced uniformity, sooner or later, is the greatest occasion of civil war, ravishing consciences, persecution of Christ Jesus in His servants, and of the hypocrisy and destruction of millions of souls."[8] Williams's viewpoint had become widely accepted by the the time of the Constitution. Benjamin Franklin, from his secular vantage point, expressed the opinion that "when a religion is good, I conceive it will support itself; and when it cannot support itself . . . so that its Professors are oblig'd to call for the help of the Civil Power, it is a sign, I apprehend, of its being a bad one."[9]

For our purposes it is important to observe that sincere believers in the Constitutional period concurred with these judgments by Williams and Franklin. With only a few exceptions, they did not want the new state and federal governments to offer official support for religion. They wanted, that is, a critical distance between the institutional life of the churches and the institutional life of the government.

A good example of that desire can be seen in the debate over Thomas Jefferson's statute for religious freedom in Virginia, which was passed in 1785. This statute made the kind of sharp break between the institutions of church and state that the First Amendment would later follow (and then in time the other state governments as well). It began with the famous words, "Whereas Almighty God hath created the mind free; that all attempts to influence it by temporal punishments or burthens, or by civil incapacitations, tend only to beget habits of hypocrisy and meanness, and are a departure from the plan of the Holy author of our religion." During debate on this law an amendment was proposed to add the words "Jesus Christ" to make it read "a departure from the plan of Jesus Christ, the holy author of our religion." Virginia's deists opposed the amendment, but so also did several members who, in the words of James Madison, "were particularly distinguished by their reputed piety and Christian zeal." The argument of these Christians against the amendment was, again as Madison summarized it, "that the better proof of reverence for that holy name would be not to profane it by making it a topic of legislative discussion, and particularly by making his religion the means of abridging the natural and equal rights of all men, in defiance of his own declaration that his Kingdom was not of this world."[10]

In other words, the Virginia Christians opposed a governmental recognition of Jesus Christ as a corruption of Christianity and a violation of God-given rights of conscience. They were groping toward the realization that the job of government was not so much to promote one religion over another as to ensure a sphere of liberty in which believers could practice their religion. It must also be said that in the Constitutional period, it was pretty much taken for granted that the practice of religion would include the exertion of an indirect influence on public policy.

A final factor moving the founders to divide institutions of church and state was the growing awareness that America might eventually become home to many people who were not of the Christian tradition. In this regard, the founders were speaking to the responsibilities of government for all of its citizens, no matter what religion they might profess. Petitions of Philadelphia Jews in the 1780s were a straw in the wind. The new Pennsylvania Constitution affirmed specifically the liberty to worship freely, but it also required officeholders in the state government to swear their belief that "the Scriptures of the old and new Testament [were] given by divine inspiration." A plaintive petition of the Philadelphia Synagogue to the government of Pennsylvania in 1783 asked if this provision was in keeping with the republican liberties secured in the Revolution. The petitioners asked "leave to represent, that in the religious books of the Jews, which are or may be in every man's hands, there are no such doctrines or principles established as are inconsistent with the safety and happiness of the people of Pennsylvania, and the conduct and behavior of the Jews in this and the neighbouring States, has always tallied with the great design of the Revolution."[11] At the federal convention in Philadelphia four years later, the delegates received a similar petition from an individual Jew, Jonas Phillips, making the same points.[12]

Whatever the precise influence of such petitions, and whatever the founders felt it was appropriate for the states to require of state officials, they made sure that Jews, Catholics, and others who did not hold to the Protestant faiths then dominant in America would be free to serve in the national government. In the words of Article VI, clause 3: "No religious Test shall ever be required as a Qualification to any Office or public Trust under the United States."

In sum, the founders' desire for the separation of the institutions of church and state reflected a desire to respect not only religion but also the moral choice of citizens. It was not a provision to remove religion as such from public life. In the context of the times it was more a device for purifying the religious impact on politics than removing it.

THE CONSTITUTION AND CHRISTIAN POLITICAL VALUES

The role of Christianity in the process that led to the Constitution is something of a puzzle. On the one hand, Christian rhetoric and organized political action by Christians were largely absent, at least by comparison with the great amount of overt Christian attention to the war with Britain. On the other hand, it is much easier to show the compatibility of basic Christian convictions with the Constitution than with the drive for independence. In addition, the governmental structure established by the Constitution seems to have provided an environment in which Christian belief and practice flourished, again in contrast to the Revolutionary period, when Christian political action led to the subversion of the faith itself.

Within the framework of Christian conviction, basic questions remain about the propriety of the American Revolution. Was it in fact a "just war"? Did it arise from necessity after the exhaustion of peaceful options for reconciliation, or was it a hasty rush to arms by a headstrong group of malcontents? Was the extravagant use of biblical typology in support of the Revolution only a pious smokescreen to hide the self-centered ambitions of the colonists?[13] Even if it is possible to answer these questions in such a way as to justify the Revolution from a Christian perspective, it takes a considerable effort. By contrast, it is easy to show the basic compatibility between important Christian convictions and certain central features of the Constitution.

Most important, the system of checks and balances established by the Constitution coincided nicely with important Christian teachings. The founders recognized, as Christians have always held, that humans are capable of great good (because made in God's image) but also of great evil (because fallen). James Madison's famous *Tenth Federalist* expressed it most clearly. Madison recognized that "the propensity of mankind, to fall into mutual animosities" arises from basic human character: the "latent causes of faction are . . . sown in the nature of man."[14] No government that overlooked this bent toward selfishness would ever succeed, no matter how noble its sentiments or lofty its aims. The republicanism of the Constitution was meant to impede this drive for selfish power while at the same time allowing citizens the freedom to fulfill more positive human desires—for peace, order, and prosperity.

Another aspect of the Constitution that comported well with Christian values requires somewhat more explanation. The Constitution was a secular document, but in the context of its time, this amounted to a virtue. The Constitution was "secular," not in the sense of repudiating religion, but in the sense of being "of this world." The founders, in other words, recognized that government was not religion and that it had the task of promoting justice and fairness on their own terms for all citizens. In fact, one of their main goals was to avoid the confusion of religious and governmental categories that had prevailed in Europe and to some extent in colonial America. This confusion had led to political tyranny through the agency of religion or religious persecution by the agents of government. It was an entanglement that, as the founders saw it, always harmed religion and always tempted authorities to exert more power than by nature and the command of God they possessed.

The contrast with the Revolution is striking. In that conflict, believers translated political differences into religious antagonisms: Support for Parliament was a sin. George Washington was Moses leading God's people out of bondage into a promised land. By the time the Constitution was written, however, there was once again a space between politics and religion. The authors of that document seemed to be saying that religion and politics occupied two different "spheres." This was not secular in the modern sense. As we have seen, there was every expectation that Christian principles would continue to play a large role in strengthening the population and even in providing a moral context for legislation. Yet the Constitution, without ever spelling it out precisely, nonetheless still acknowledges that the functions of government in society have a different role than the functions of religion. Both are important, and important to each other. But they are different. It might even be argued that the authors of the Constitution were inching toward an acknowledgment of both the dignity of the political "sword" and the integrity of the Christian "kingdom" (to use phrases from Luther).

In sum, the Constitution was realistic about human nature, and it was cautious about the role of government, especially over against the role of the churches. In these areas the Constitution came up very well to Christian teachings. Humans were fallen and did need to be restrained in the pursuit of power. God had established government with its own beneficent purposes.

To recognize the ways in which the Constitution comported well with Christian beliefs is not to claim that a special divine miracle lay behind its ratification. It is rather to say that the path from the Revolution to the Constitution, a journey that involved both expansion of revolutionary principles and their restriction, led Americans, both believers and many influential leaders who were not Christians in a conventional sense, to a Constitution that conformed roughly to general Christian principles. This is by no means the whole story, for there were certain elements of the Constitution that can also be questioned from a Christian point of view (for some of these, see appendix B), but it is significant, especially when considering the absence of overt Christian action in the process of Constitution-writing itself.

PRACTICAL RESULTS

It is difficult to draw sure connections between political activities and the internal life of the churches. Nonetheless, it does seem as if the vitality of Christianity in America declined during the Revolutionary period and began to revive during the 1790s.[15] The difficulties of the churches in the earlier period stemmed in part from the war itself—congregations disrupted, finances in disarray, attention monopolized by news of battle, and so forth. But other matters came into play as well. The long slide of the New England heirs of the Puritans into Unitarianism, the aggressive promotion of deistic religion by leaders of the Revolution like Tom Paine and Ethan Allen, and the massive migration into the unsettled "West" (Kentucky and Tennessee in that period)—all these developments sapped the vitality of traditional belief.

In addition, however, the intense Christian involvement in the war effort also curtailed Christian energies. With the level of Christian commitment to the patriot cause so high, it is hard to believe that energies normally devoted to Christian causes were not being diverted.

The recovery of Christianity after the Revolution was steady in the 1790s and then dramatic after the turn of the century. By 1800 or shortly thereafter a pattern of revivals was established in the West, in the less settled areas of New England, and along the Atlantic coast. Within another twenty years, active revivalism was matched by the active promotion of reform. The combination of concern for revival and creation of reform societies led to the spread of the churches and significant "Christianization" of the culture. The causes that led to these effects will probably never be entirely clear. Psychological needs related to the rapidly changing character of American society, connections with new forms of economic organization, the charisma of the new nation's religious leaders, the increasingly widespread desire to shape the society by biblical norms—all played a role, in addition to which Christian may wish to add the sovereign work of God's Spirit.[16]

Along with these other causes for Christian expansion may be added the possibility that a certain Christian retreat from overt political activity may also have played a role. As we will see in the following chapters, that retreat was never complete. American Christians continued to follow the "Reformed" pattern in politics. Yet the Constitution and related developments in the states did succeed in creating a certain space between religion and politics. Modern historians have pointed out that Christian expansion in the early United States occurred most dramatically after believers turned from reliance upon overt political means to the organization of voluntary societies.[17] James Madison testified to the same end when, as an old man, he wrote about the condition of religion in Virginia since 1785 and the proclamation of absolute religious liberty in the state: "I cannot speak particularly of any of the cases excepting that of Virg[inia] where it is impossible to deny that Religion prevails with more zeal, and a more exemplary priesthood than it ever did when established and patronised by public authority. We are teaching the world the great truth that Govts. do better without Kings & Nobles than with them. The merit will be doubled by the other lesson that Religion flourishes in greater purity, without than with the aid of Govt."[18]

Lyman Beecher, the leader of Connecticut's Congregationalists, came to the same conclusion. After first vigorously opposing the disestablishment of the Congregational church in his state, he came to accept the disestablishment that occurred in 1818, and even to regard it as a great blessing for the churches. Now freed of entanglements with the state, the church could be more energetic about its proper tasks of proclaiming the gospel and doing deeds of mercy.[19]

These statements must not be pressed. Madison and Beecher were not speaking about the withdrawal of religion from public life, but only about the much more specific separation between the institutions of the church and the institutions of the state. In addition, both probably thought that the ardent religious support for the Revolution had been acceptable. Still, their testimony and the general religious history of the period suggest that, on balance, political activity by Christian during the Revolution was not particularly advantageous to Christianity itself, whereas the effect of the Constitution was, if not favorable, then at least not unfavorable, to the growth and integrity of Christianity.

COMPARING THE REVOLUTIONARY AND CONSTITUTIONAL PERIODS

Such a conclusion brings us back to the apparent paradox. When Christian involvement was intense—during the Revolution—Christianity suffered. When Christian involvement was much less intense—during the writing of the Constitution—the results were better for the faith. A snap judgment might be that the lesson here is to abandon political activity in order to preserve Christian faith. But that is much too fast. The crucial variable may not be political involvement or its absence, but the kind of political involvement, the nature of political activity, characteristic of the two periods.

The political process leading to the Constitution featured several elements absent from the earlier religious involvement in the Revolution. First was the importance for the authors of the Constitution of a theory of government. Questions may remain about whether the

Constitution is the best possible form of government. At the least, however, it may be said that the Constitution was more than a republican reflex or spasm. For Madison and several other important founders it represented the application of careful political principle to the lived experience of Americans.

Second, the political theory lying behind the Constitution was complex in a way that mirrored, to some extent, the complexity of human experience itself. The founders had come to see, for example, that reaction against traditional abuses of power can lead to new ways of abusing power. To use modern jargon, they were aware of the ironic potential in human experience. They had come to sense that good solutions to pressing problems regularly create new problems of their own. This simple recognition was by no means a panacea, but it did protect the founders from the disillusionment that so often attends crusades. Crusades usually fail, but crusaders stand in even greater risk when they succeed, for the result is inevitably disappointment that achievements cannot live up to anticipations. The authors of the Constitution, in other words, had learned a lesson taught not only by human experience but also by centuries of theological reflection on the central teachings of Christianity.

Third, the Constitution was a product of considerable compromise. Its authors worked toward definite goals (not always compatible) but still found it possible to compromise with one another. If there had been an all-or-nothing mentality at Philadelphia, there would have been no Constitution.

Finally, the Constitution restored a certain distance between religion and politics. This distance has little to do with modern questions of church and state, although the religious provisions of the First Amendment are an important indication of that distance. Thomas Jefferson was a lonely radical with his belief that a total barrier should be erected between religion and politics. Madison was closer to the mainstream with his belief that voluntarily supported religious activities may take their place in public life. And Justice Joseph Story, author of the era's most influential commentaries on the Constitution, was even more typical in the early republic. Story believed that "the promulgation of the great doctrines of religion . . . can never be a matter of indifference to any well ordered community. . . . Indeed, in a republic, there would seem to be a peculiar propriety in viewing the Christian religion, as the great basis, on which it must rest for its support and permanence, if it be, what it has been deemed by its truest friends to be, the religion of liberty."[20]

In other words, the issue in the early republic was not separation of religion and public life as we know the problem today. It was, rather, the question of critical distance. That distance was lost in the Revolutionary period, and the result was harmful for Christianity. It was regained during the Constitutional period—partly as a result of the Constitution itself—and the result for Christianity itself was much more propitious.

One last historical observation is pertinent for this early period in America's national life. The American record of Christian involvement in politics seems to be marked by its pulsations. Among Christians, bursts of fervent political activity alternate with periods of political withdrawal. Whether such a pattern is endemic to America's "Reformed" approach to politics, and whether there might be more to gain from a simultaneous combination of engagement and withdrawal are questions to be considered as we proceed. Now, to illustrate that persistent oscillation, we turn to the election of 1800, when American Christians again returned with a vengeance to the fray.

5. The Campaign of 1800: Fire Without Light

The presidential election of 1800 was a major religious event. Not until 1928, when the Roman Catholicism of candidate Al Smith became a major issue, and then again in very recent years, was religion so obviously important in a presidential contest. In 1800 the focus of concern was Thomas Jefferson of Virginia, candidate of the Democratic-Republicans, who was contending for the presidency against the incumbent, Federalist John Adams of Massachusetts. The heart of religious concern was the fear that the nation would come to grief if the "infidel" Jefferson were elected. Those who expressed this concern were almost exclusively evangelical Protestants. Moreover, they were not insignificant persons on the fringes but some of the country's leading Christian spokesmen.

This relatively minor incident in the nation's political history is yet unusually instructive for modern people of faith. It illustrates something of the complexity of the political process, and also something of what is necessary to distinguish superficial political knowledge from genuine wisdom. It shows the dangers of bringing a single-issue mentality to an election campaign, the advantages of a full analysis of a candidate's positions, and the religious hazards of a complete identification with a contending political faction. It is, in sum, a cautionary tale. Like the story itself, its moral is complex, explaining not only the dangers of overcommitment to a political cause but also the dangers of withdrawal from the political process.

THE OPPOSITION TO JEFFERSON

The opponents of Jefferson included such prominent New England Congregationalists as Timothy Dwight, president of Yale College, and

Jedidiah Morse of Massachusetts, a leading promoter of theological education, foreign missions, and the dissemination of the Bible. Evangelical clergymen in New York such as the Scottish Presbyterian John Mitchell Mason and the Dutch Reformed William Linn echoed the concerns of their Congregational brethren to the north. Presbyterians from New Jersey, including the president of Princeton, Samuel Stanhope Smith, and one of the most active Christian laymen in the country, Elias Boudinot, expressed a similar foreboding for the nation's future if Jefferson were to win the election.

These evangelicals feared Jefferson for several reasons, all of which seemed to make the prospect of his election a horror. In the first place, Jefferson had led the fight in Virginia for the disestablishment of the Anglican church immediately after the American Revolution. Evangelical Congregationalists in New England saw this move as an assault upon religion altogether, for their denomination was still established by law in both Connecticut and Massachusetts. To them this establishment was but the necessary recognition that societies needed to acknowledge and heed the will of God. Evangelicals in New York and New Jersey were not committed to establishment, but they resented the way in which Jefferson had appeared to belittle all religion when he had spoken out for disestablishment in his own state.

Particularly galling to these evangelicals were statements Jefferson had made in his *Notes on Virginia,* published in 1784. There, Jefferson seemed to dismiss the importance of Christian belief in favor of a radical kind of freedom. "It does me no injury," Jefferson had written, "for my neighbor to say there are twenty gods, or no God. It neither picks my pocket nor breaks my leg." Jefferson instead put his trust in "reason and free inquiry," for these were "the only effectual agents against error." Such statements, and the flippant spirit evinced by some of Jefferson's other comments (e.g., "the happy discovery, that the way to silence religious disputes, is to take no notice of them"), seemed to indicate that Jefferson opposed religion itself as much as its establishment.[1]

To be sure, Jefferson's stand on church and state had won him the support of a few Baptists and a small number of other evangelicals who opposed a religious establishment on principle. But their influence was much less than that exerted by the presidents of the country's two most prestigious evangelical colleges (Yale's Dwight and Princeton's Smith) and the most visible leaders of interdenominational cooperation (Morse of Massachusetts and Boudinot of New Jersey).

Jefferson himself was always reticent about making his religious beliefs public. He was a member in good standing of his local Episcopal church in Virginia, and later in life he even contributed to a Bible society. Yet rumors had spread of his unorthodox views. It was said that he so highly exalted reason that he had no place for divine revelation. Another widely circulated suspicion was that Jefferson did not believe in the deity of Christ, but rather held him simply to be an extraordinarily good man. Although nothing definite could be said about these matters in 1800 (they happened substantially to represent Jefferson's actual beliefs), enough information was abroad to make some Christians very uneasy.

Yet another cause for concern was Jefferson's connection with France. He had served as an ambassador to that country for several years and had made no secret of his admiration for the French *philosophes* and for the general course of the French Revolution. Even when that revolution turned to bloody excess and when many other Americans began to repudiate it, Jefferson continued to support those Frenchmen who wanted to rid themselves of the fetters of the past. To many Protestants in America, Jefferson's fondness for things French told volumes about his own instability. In their minds France was the country where a prostitute had been crowned Goddess of Reason at the cathedral of Notre Dame. It was the place where unchecked violence had first overthrown settled government, then executed the ruling family, and at last given way to the dictatorship of Napoleon Bonaparte. Anyone who professed to find *this* attractive was a threat to his own country.

A third reason many evangelicals feared Jefferson was that he represented the political opposition. During George Washington's first term as president (1789–93), political leaders had succeeded in preserving the vision of nonpartisanship born during the Revolution. But in Washington's second term and during the tenure of John Adams (1797–1801), great infighting had broken loose.[2] Political factionalism returned to

America with a vengeance. Democratic-Republicans contended for liberty and the people; the Federalists were loud in defense of order and security. To those Protestants who were also Federalists, Jefferson as the leader of the Democratic-Republicans had to bear the responsibility for destroying the harmony of the republic. Faction, partisanship, discord, turmoil—all seemed to be the responsibility of the upstarts who clamored for states' rights, liberty, and the freedoms of the people. (Democratic-Republicans, it is hardly necessary to add, felt that the cause of public strife was the high-handedness of the Federalists, represented most strikingly by the repressive Alien and Sedition Acts that had been passed during President Adams's tenure.)

These then were the reasons many evangelical leaders feared Jefferson. As they saw him, he was a foe to the public influence of religion. He was suspect in his own personal beliefs. He was contaminated by the irreligion and disorder of France. And he was responsible for the great degeneration in American public life.

A RELIGIOUS CAMPAIGN

As the country moved closer to 1800, the evangelical Protestants went into action to make their views on Jefferson known. On the Fourth of July in 1798, Timothy Dwight spoke out against the party of Jefferson by linking Democratic-Republicans explicitly to the atheistic movements of France. "For what end shall we be connected with men of whom this is the character and conduct? . . . Is it that our churches may become temples of reason . . . and our psalms of praise Marseilles hymns? Is it that we may change our holy worship into a dance of Jacobin frenzy and that we may behold a strumpet impersonating a Goddess on the altars of Jehovah?"[3]

As the election came closer, concern grew more intense. John Mitchell Mason posed the terms very starkly in the election year itself: "Fellow Christians—A crisis of no common magnitude awaits our country. The approaching election of a president is to decide a question not merely of preference to an eminent individual, or particular views of policy, but, what is infinitely more, of national regard or disregard to the religion of Jesus Christ. . . . I dread the election of Mr. Jefferson, because I believe him to be a confirmed infidel."[4]

A similar appeal came from William Linn in a pamphlet titled *Serious Considerations on the Election of a President*. Linn denied that he was seeking political influence for himself but made no bones about his intent to demonstrate Jefferson's unfitness for national office. Linn reviewed Jefferson's beliefs as found in the *Notes on the State of Virginia* and also provided other quotations from Jefferson to show his dangerous beliefs. As Linn saw it, Jefferson's professed respect for Jesus was merely a sham, since the Virginian was a mere deist (that is, one who believed in a distant, watchmaker God) and as such no better than an atheist. Linn foresaw dire consequences if Jefferson were elected: Other nations would scorn the new United States for showing so little respect for traditional Christianity. Society would decline still further into immorality. And most dreadful, God himself would be offended and return to judge the nation.[5]

Shortly before the states began to vote, the Federalist *Gazette of the United States* added its religious conclusions. Its ultimatum summarized the evangelical Federalist case against Jefferson: "THE GRAND QUESTION STATED: At the present solemn moment the only question to be asked by every American, laying his hand on his heart, is 'Shall I continue in allegiance to GOD AND A RELIGIOUS PRESIDENT [John Adams] or impiously declare for JEFFERSON AND NO GOD!!!' "[6]

A CONSPIRACY THEORY

The last fear hanging over the heads of these leaders was that Jefferson might be the agent of an atheistic conspiracy. At the end of the century some of America's denominational leaders were very concerned about the general state of society. The Presbyterian General Assembly, meeting in May 1798, spoke, for example, of Europe beset by "destruction to morals and religion . . . and . . . our own country . . . threatened with similar calumnies." In such a situation, "insensibility in us would be stupidity; silence would be criminal."[7] In early June of that same year the Congregational clergy of New England made a similar declaration. Soon leading evangelical ministers thought they had discovered the source of the trouble.

First Jedidiah Morse and then Timothy Dwight proclaimed the

existence of a vast conspiracy, called the Bavarian Illuminati, that they supposed was reaching its tentacles into the United States. Morse and Dwight were availing themselves of detailed exposés from the continent that had identified the Illuminati as the source of most of the public evil that had occurred in Europe for the past century.[8] Now they felt that the combination of godlessness and disorder spreading over the United States was a sign that the agents of this conspiracy were abroad in the land. And since they linked the "leveling" (or democratic) ideas and the French Revolution to this conspiracy, it was only natural that they saw Jefferson as the agent, witting or unwitting, of this cabal.

By the time of the actual voting in 1800, doubt had been cast on the Illuminati theory, but numerous evangelical leaders still believed that such an evil conspiracy was a genuine threat. In this Morse and Dwight were joined by some of the Presbyterians, including Samuel Stanhope Smith.

As it turned out, the election saw the triumph of the Democratic-Republicans over the Federalists. Because of gliches in the Constitution's original provision for national elections, however, the Democratic-Republican candidates for president (Jefferson) and vice president (Aaron Burr) ended in a tie for the nation's highest office in the electoral college. This caused considerable wrangling among the victors and momentary pleasure among the defeated. But the Christian Federalists were largely depressed. Of the selection between Jefferson and Burr, Elias Boudinot could only bemoan that the choice for president now lay "between two such great evils. Alas! for my country."[9]

Immediately after Jefferson's victory, some of those who had opposed him on religious grounds felt that the worst was just around the corner. Princeton's President Smith, for instance, held that Jefferson was promoting policies leading to "national imbecility and disorganization" and that he was encouraging "turbulence and anarchy" by delivering the nation "from one hotheaded and furious faction to another, till we are torn asunder."[10] Elias Boudinot could only shake his head and conclude that "nothing short of fatal experience, will open the Eyes of the deluded Multitudes."[11]

COUNTERARGUMENT: POLITICAL AND RELIGIOUS

By no means all Christians in 1800 saw the situation as these opponents of Jefferson did. Members of the more populist denominations like the Baptists and the Methodists were often in Jefferson's camp. An Episcopal clergyman, John Cosens Ogden, even attempted to reverse the charge. He suggested that the Illuminati scare was nothing but a conspiracy of the *Federalists* and their clerical allies to prejudice the people against the Jeffersonians.[12]

Other Christians objected not so much to the political stances in the campaign as to the way political activity was overwhelming more directly Christian concerns. Dr. Benjamin Rush, a noted Philadelphia physician, was a sincere if freethinking believer who felt that clergymen were going too far. His views on the matter, as expressed in a letter to Jefferson in October 1800, are worth quoting at length, in part because they were so similar to the opinions of the Reverend Ezra Stiles during the Revolution.

Were it possible for St. Paul to rise from his grave at the present juncture, he would say to the Clergy who are now so active in settling the political Affairs of the World: "Cease from your political labors—your kingdom is not of *this* World. Read my Epistles. In no part of them will you perceive me aiming to depose a pagan Emperor, or to place a Christian upon a throne. Christianity disdains to receive Support from human Governments. From this, it derives its preeminence over all the religions that ever have, or ever shall exist in the World. Human Governments may receive Support from Christianity but it must be only from the love of justice, and peace which is calculated to produce in the minds of men. By promoting these, and all the other Christian virtues by your precepts, and example, you will much sooner overthrow errors of all kind, and establish our pure and holy religion in the world, than by aiming to produce by your preaching, or pamphlets any thing in the political State of mankind."

Rush then went on to tell a story about a minister who, as he saw it, acted more wisely. The setting was England in the 1640s, when many clergymen played an active role in supporting Oliver Cromwell and the Parliamentary opposition to the king.

A certain Dr. Owen, an eminent minister of the Gospel among the dissenters in England, and a sincere friend to liberty, was once complained of by one of Cromwell's time serving priests, that he did not preach to the *times*. "My business and duty," said the disciple of St. Paul, "is to preach, to *Eternity*, not to the *times*."[13]

Rush may have exaggerated the apolitical character of the Apostle Paul's message, but he did have a point to make in the highly charged religious atmosphere of 1800.

A few Congregationalists in Timothy Dwight's Connecticut shared Rush's concern. At the height of the campaign, the Hartford North Association advised clergymen to "exercise great candor, moderation and prudence, and avoid such an interference as shall tend to destroy their usefulness as ministers of the gospel."[14] Like Rush, they saw difficulties ahead if the Christian faith became too political.

For his part, Jefferson completely turned the tables. The behavior of his political opponents, who used Christianity (as Jefferson saw it) to protect their own wealth and influence, was simply unchristian. Such behavior only added another episode to the sorry history of perversions by Christians of the pure morals of Jesus. Jefferson summed up his opinions on the matter to a correspondent in 1810:

The purest system of morals ever before preached to man has been adulterated and sophisticated, by artificial constructions, into a mere contrivance to filch wealth and power to themselves, [so] that rational men[,] not being able to swallow their impious heresies, in order to force them down their throats, they raise the hue and cry of infidelity, while themselves are the greatest obstacles to the advancement of the real doctrines of Jesus, and do in fact constitute the real Anti-Christ.[15]

Needless to say, Jefferson's Christian opponents in 1800 hardly appreciated such a sentiment.

INCONSISTENCIES AND IRONIES

No one can doubt the sincerity of the Christians who opposed Jefferson, nor can they be faulted for their desire to promote godliness in the public sphere. They were also approximately correct in their assessment of Jefferson's own religious beliefs. He was not, by any stretch of the imagination, an orthodox Christian. And he valued Christian churches mostly for their role in preserving public morality. It is certainly true as well that evangelical leaders saw correctly some of the dangers in Jefferson's political convictions. His educational theories, for example, had no place for religious influence but promoted a deceptive ideal of intellectual neutrality.

All this having been said, the great religious outcry against Jefferson was both inconsistent and quite ironical. It was inconsistent because Jefferson's opponents failed to apply their exacting religious standards to their own candidates. And it was ironical because the "infidel" Jefferson actually stands among the most moral and upright presidents in the history of the United States.

In the first instance, Federalists who opposed Jefferson for his heterodoxy failed to apply the same standards to their own candidate. Though John Adams, like Jefferson, did not display his religion on his sleeve, his actual convictions were very close to Jefferson's. John Adams's wife, Abigail, was orthodox in belief and practice, but he was more of a conservative deist. Like Jefferson, Adams belittled the Christian reverence for Scripture, once writing his son John Quincy in reproof for the younger Adams's belief that one could find *the* scriptural solution to a problem. And like Jefferson, he held that the idea of an Incarnation was simply nonsense.

In addition, the Christian opponents of Jefferson failed to assess their party's own political tactics with the rigor that they applied to those of the Democratic-Republicans. Federalist political forces included some who took the high road but many who were willing to fight it out in the gutter. In this they were little better or worse than the Democratic-Republicans. The simple inconsistency was that Christian scruples seemed to stop at the boundary of party affiliation. What was a cause for scandal and alarm in the opponent aroused virtually no comment when it appeared in an ally.

Much more important for modern consideration is the larger irony that attends the Christian opposition to Jefferson. His administration turned out to have a moral tone and to promote policies that, in several crucial areas, comported very well with basic Christian values. In matters of personal rectitude, Jefferson was scrupulous, for example, in accounting for federal funds. He also conducted himself with great probity in the dispensation of patronage, an area that regularly called up the worst in both applicant and executive. In this he differed dramatically from Alexander Hamilton of the Federalists and Aaron Burr of his own party, two statesmen who regularly used political patronage to enhance their own prestige or increase their own wealth. Jefferson, by contrast, went out of his way to act honorably with the funds and personnel entrusted to his care. He was in debt when he died, not because he was profligate with his means, but because he had put the public good ahead of private gain.

Apart from matters of personal honesty, Jefferson's policies were also generally moral. He sustained in Washington the effort he had made in Virginia to ensure freedom of religious expression for all and to prevent the state from imposing one form of religious belief or another on its citizens. This was but a specific instance of his conviction that governmental intrusion into ordinary life was dangerous. Throughout his career Jefferson was an advocate of less government rather than more. He did not despise the accomplishments of organized politics, but he felt that the great powers potentially available to government made it a likely candidate for corruption. In this the Enlightenment thinker (who otherwise had an optimistic view of human nature) displayed a greater degree of Christian realism than the believers among his opponents (who often talked as if governmental aid for the churches and large-scale governmental activities were both unalloyed blessings).

JEFFERSON AND WAR

Perhaps most strikingly, Jefferson also showed a Christian respect for life. The most obvious example here was his great reluctance to commit the nation to war. During his administration, tensions with both France and England were often high. As a consequence there were voices in both major parties insisting on war as a way to defend the national honor. Many patriots felt that only the field of battle could bring vindication against England's high-handed dominance of the sea, or against France's attacks on American shipping. Jefferson was not a pacifist, but he nonetheless was deeply opposed to warfare, except as a last resort. And so he resisted these appeals and tried to find peaceful alternatives to resolve international conflicts. After his term as president, Jefferson went so far as to point out how close his policies came to the "principles *professed* by the Friends [i.e., Quakers]." Although the Quakers of Pennsylvania were among Jefferson's most determined political foes, he was not reluctant to claim that "our efforts to preserve peace, our measures as to the Indians, as to slavery, as to religious freedom, were all in consonance with their *professions.*"[16] Once again, Jefferson himself was asking to be judged not by an externally imposed standard of doctrine but an internally derived measure of behavior.

Jefferson's most explicit pursuit of peaceful internal politics involved the Embargo Act. This was an effort to force Britain and France to negotiate with the United States by closing American ports to all shipping, foreign and domestic. The occasion for this policy was a blatant act of British aggression on America's very shores. In late June 1807, the British warship *Leopard* attacked an American ship, the *Chesapeake,* as the American vessel was clearing the harbor at Norfolk, Virginia. The British were looking for deserters from their navy, but the unprovoked assault upon the American ship, which resulted in twenty-one casualties, was a recognized justification for war. Against the outcry for immediate retaliation, Jefferson pursued a course of deliberate procrastination. Finally, he acted late in the year by encouraging Congress to pass the Embargo Act. His purpose in all of this was to avoid the slaughter that battle entailed, even in that day of wooden warships and single-shot muskets.

Historians and political scientists have long been divided concerning the success of the Embargo Act. In its actual outworking it brought greater economic hardship to American merchants than to either the British or the French. And Jefferson was not entirely successful in cooling tensions. Still, his efforts were a partial success. He had shown that it was possible at least to attempt peaceful means of solving international conflicts. And he had demonstrated that a president could cool passionate nationalistic ardor. Many historians today feel that when war with Britain did come in 1812, under the leadership of

President James Madison, it was a needless conflict that could have been avoided with only a little more of the restraint that marked Jefferson's handling of the earlier crisis.

In sum, the individual whom evangelicals had feared as an "infidel" turned out to be not only an honest president but a president whose policies reflected at least general agreement with basic Christian values. This is not to say that Jefferson was more moral than Adams or even that his policies were always more in line with biblical values. It is, however, to say that the great fears of Jefferson's opponents in 1798, 1799, and 1800 were misplaced. They had misread the man and the times as well.

LESSONS

A number of observations from the history of 1800 are pertinent at the end of the twentieth century. But first, it is important to say what the earlier story does *not* mean: It does not mean that Christian involvement in politics should cease. Nor does it mean that Christians are doing something illegitimate when they assess candidates and issues by moral and religious criteria. Soon after the election of 1800, in fact, most American Christians did turn more generally aside from political involvement. It was as if they were being doubly cautious in light of their mistakes in assessing the issues in 1800. This, however, was unfortunate. Public issues of great complexity and deep moral importance still faced the new country. Issues like states' rights and slavery were crying out for consistent Christian consideration. Christians did much good in the first half of the nineteenth century in evangelism, moral reform, and mission efforts, but they did not contribute a great deal to the political process. The nation was the poorer for it.

The lessons to be learned from the anti-Jeffersonian fear deal rather with *how* Christians are to be involved politically. Here at least three matters are important.

The first of these concerns the damage done to the church when Christians identify their cause completely with a single political party, position, or person. It simply was not the case that Jefferson and the Democratic-Republicans were the quintessence of evil, nor Adams and the Federalists the paradigm of virtue. Given the basic Christian teachings on human nature—that the redeemed can still act as sinners and that sinners can still contribute to public good—Christians in 1800 should have realized that a mixture of good and evil would be found in both parties. To be sure, certain policies of either one may have been more or less Christian than policies of the other. But this did not release believers from the responsibility of speaking realistically about the Christian character of the candidates they favored and those whom they opposed. When they did identify the Christian cause with only one party, they undermined both the faith and the political process.

Second, the story of 1800 should remind us that Christian activity in politics needs to include examination of public positions as well as of personal beliefs. Even if Jefferson had been an unbeliever, his policies would have deserved consideration in their own right. It is at least arguable that his public actions came closer to meeting biblical standards than those of the Federalists whom the evangelical leaders supported. On the matter of individual liberties, for example, Jefferson recognized more clearly than his opponents that governmental meddling can lead to the abuse of religion even more than to its support. Given the American circumstances and the actual nature of the current threat, the Federalists' alien and sedition acts were an assault on liberty that did not comport well with Christian principles. Jefferson's restraint on warfare showed a more consistent appreciation for the value of human life than did the policies of those Federalists who were eager to go to war. In a similar way, Jefferson realized that no ultimate questions of justice or national self-existence were at stake in disputes with France or England, so he sought peaceful solutions. In this he again acted in accord with general Christian principles.

The critics of Jefferson would have seen this more easily if they had gone beyond mere reaction against his religious beliefs to an actual analysis of his public record. Before the election of 1800, Jefferson had served as governor of Virginia, as the first United States secretary of state, and also as John Adams's vice president. In each of these positions he had instituted programs that showed a remarkable discernment concerning the potential evils of overweening government. And in each he evidenced a consistent respect for human life and dignity. As governor of Virginia he had worked to protect the rights of religious minorities (mostly evangelical Baptists and Presbyterians in the back-country) who were not members of the Episcopal church. As Washington's secretary of state in the early 1790s he had displayed considerable skill in promoting the interests of the United States against Britain, France, and Spain, while proceeding cautiously to avoid war.

The point here is that political programs deserve independent assessment. It will not do to dismiss public policies simply because they come from someone who lacks religious credentials, nor to embrace policies because they come wrapped in God-talk. Closer and more substantial analysis is required. Often in American political history, those who use Christian language have in fact taken positions that accord well with Christian values—but not always, and never consistently.

Finally, the history of this episode constitutes a fresh reminder about the complexity of the political process. Though certain issues will be more important at some political moments than at others, issues are interrelated. Though certain leaders may indeed be more genuinely Christian than others, their policies almost inevitably contain a mixture of values—decidedly Christian, decidedly non-Christian, and (usually) the largest percentage open to divergent interpretation. In the election of 1800, believers probably were correct to worry about Jefferson's ideological commitment to democracy and his disrespect for political and religious traditions. Yet if they had gone on to analyze other issues with the same religious care, they may have discovered that other aspects of Jefferson's record coincided much more closely with Christian values. It was not a mistake to judge Jefferson's commitment to democracy by religious standards; it was a mistake to let a judgment on one part of his record overwhelm concern for the whole.

Christian thinkers through the centuries have recognized in a general way the nature of human complexity. The Apostle Paul spoke eloquently in the Scriptures themselves when he described how his own motives were mixed in approaching questions of good and evil (Romans 7). Martin Luther during the Reformation described the Christian as one who was "at the same time a justified person and a sinner." Others looking at the more recent past have demonstrated how God is able to accomplish his purposes as he stands hidden behind the mistakes of his children and the evil intents of his enemies.

Despite this lengthy Christian tradition, the failure to recognize the complexity of politics has proven a persistent difficulty in American religious history. Yet because politics partakes of the human condition, and because humanity is complex, Christians do well to approach political issues with careful analysis, with a distrust of their first impressions, and with a commitment to explore as many sides of an issue as possible. Here the words of Elton Trueblood are appropriate: "One of the best contributions which Christian thought can make to the thought of the world is the repetition that life is complex. It is part of the Christian understanding of reality that all simplistic answers to basic questions are bound to be false. Over and over, the answer is both-and rather than either-or."

With the hindsight of history it is possible to say that the evangelical Protestant leaders of 1800 saw some political things clearly and some with distortion. They were courageous in bearing witness to God amidst the give-and-take of the political marketplace, but they would have done better if they had applied their religious values more thoughtfully to the issues of the day. Their difficulty was not the application of Christian values to the political process, it was doing so with more courage than intelligence, more fire than light.

6. The Transcendent Faith of Abraham Lincoln

The religion of Abraham Lincoln has always been a perplexing topic, especially in relation to his politics. Since Lincoln is one of the great mythic figures in American history, the whole subject is prone to pious oversimplification and partisan exploitation. The reality of Lincoln's faith—what it was and how it changed throughout his life—is, however, too important to be left to the mythmakers.

That reality is doubly important for our purposes. First, it illustrates one of the central paradoxes of America's religious-political history, which, although complicated in application, can be stated simply. As we have seen, the strong view of Christian America is misguided—America has no more claim to a special relationship with God than other nations do. At the same time, however, belief in the divine mission of the United States has inspired many Americans—including Abraham Lincoln—to public service of a profoundly Christian character and to political activity deeply colored by moral considerations. The paradox is that such a potentially harmful view of the nation can inspire such praiseworthy public service.

Lincoln's religion is also important for American political history because of its own inner character. By the lights of both his contemporaries and later Christian, Lincoln's beliefs were deficient and substandard. Nonetheless, the faith of this individual, the raw woodsman become a busy lawyer, turns out to reveal religious depths largely unknown among his more conventionally pious peers.

The role of religious faith in Lincoln's political vision and, even more, the character of that faith itself are the themes of this chapter. Unlike the Federalist campaigners in the election of 1800, who compromised religion by subsuming it to the political needs of the moment, Lincoln exercised a faith that, by transcending the moment, preserved both political effect and spiritual power.

DEBATE OVER LINCOLN'S RELIGION

The confusion over Lincoln's religion comes about from its multiple ambiguities. On the one hand, Lincoln was, in the words of biographers James Randall and Richard Current, "a man of more intense religiosity than any other President the United States has ever had."[1] Lincoln's piety and his seriousness about his responsibilities under God are attested by the most unshakable evidence, including a large number of statements from his own pen.

On the other hand, Lincoln's faith was not conventional. As a young man in Illinois he read the freethinkers Paine and Volney with appreciation, and he always gave an Enlightenment style of reasoning a primary place in his approach to the world. At the same time, moreover, he was a kind of "frontier spiritualist" who believed that signs, dreams, and portents foretold the future. He had no use for Christian creeds or statements of faith, and little use for formal theology.[2]

Lincoln probably was also a Universalist who believed in the eventual salvation of all people. And although he spoke of God very often and in many different ways (William J. Wolf counted thirty-three different expressions, like "Almighty Being" or "Father of Mercies," in the *Collected Works*), Lincoln rarely referred to Jesus. After the death of his four-year-old son, Edward, in 1850, he regularly attended Presbyterian churches in Springfield and Washington pastored by doctrinal conservatives. Yet he never became a member of any congregation.

An incident early in his political career highlights the unconventional character of Lincoln's faith. When in 1846 he stood for election to Congress from Illinois's Seventh Congressional District, the rumor began to spread that he mocked Christianity and scoffed at religious practice. Given the circumstances of the race, this amounted to a vital issue, since Lincoln's opponent was a Methodist circuit-riding preacher, Peter Cartwright, a man widely known for his piety. To quiet the alarm Lincoln published a broadside on his religion that denied any wrongdoing. Significantly, however, it made little claim to anything positive. The key part of Lincoln's circular went like this:

A charge having got into circulation in some of the neighborhoods of this District, in substance that I am an open scoffer at Christianity, I have by the

advice of some friends concluded to notice the subject in this form. That I am
not a member of any Christian Church, is true; but I have never denied the
truth of the Scriptures; and I have never spoken with intentional disrespect
of religion in general, or of any denomination of Christians in particular.
. . . I do not think I could myself, be brought to support a man for office,
whom I knew to be an open enemy of, and scoffer at, religion. Leaving the
higher matter of eternal consequences, between him and his Maker, I still do
not think any man has the right thus to insult the feelings, and injure the
morals, of the community in which he may live.[3]

Even as he recognized the importance of religious propriety for public
officials, Lincoln still made clear that his religion was very much his
own business.

Lincoln's manifest trust in God alongside his unconventional piety
confounded contemporaries. One of the most popular early biographies
was a book by Joseph Gilbert Holland, published in 1866, that described
Lincoln as a model evangelical gentleman. This effort greatly offended
Lincoln's Springfield law partner, William Herndon, who thought he
knew what Lincoln was really like. The portrait that emerged in
Herndon's own biographical study was much saltier. In that book,
Lincoln appeared as a prairie "infidel" who got along very well without the church, an amibtious, even scheming, politician, a man more
fond of the bawdy than the Bible, more given to introspective melancholy than to Christian holiness.

Since the time of Holland and Herndon, the battle has gone on
unabated. In the 1870s and 1880s, the question of Lincoln's religion was
a focus of political squabbling. Democrats often painted Lincoln as an
impious conniver in order to undermine Republican efforts at recon-
structing the South. Republicans, in turn, transformed Lincoln into a
saintly Christian patriot in order to lend greater dignity to the Reconstruction they linked with his name.

Modern studies continue the contrast. In G. Frederick Owen's *Abraham Lincoln: The Man and His Faith* (published in 1976 and reprinted
several times), Lincoln appears as a Christian prophet who sustained
consistent evangelical convictions throughout his life. In Gore Vidal's
Lincoln, by contrast, Christianity is a superfluous veneer that Lincoln
occasionally paraded for political purposes.

Nonetheless, it is possible to get a clearer picture of Lincoln and his faith. But it must come from the sober histories, careful biographies like those by Benjamin Thomas, Stephen B. Oates, and James Randall, the definitive *Collected Works of Abraham Lincoln,* the specialized studies that disentangle legend from history (such as Oates's recent and very helpful *Abraham Lincoln: The Man Behind the Myths*), and the well-documented and carefully nuanced studies of Lincoln's faith itself (of which the best is William Wolf's *The Almost Chosen People*).[4]

THE CIRCUMSTANCES OF LINCOLN'S RELIGION

The greatest difficulty in coming to a unified picture of Lincoln's faith is that his religion, with its sensibilities and practice, does not fit into modern categories. He was not an orthodox, evangelical, "born-again" Christian striving toward the "higher life" (as these terms have been used since the 1870s). But neither was he a skeptical "modernist" with a prejudice against the supernatural and an aversion to the Bible.

Three historical circumstances help explain the nature of Lincoln's faith. First, he grew up as a member of a poor dirt-farming family in the upper South and lower Midwest without privilege, position, or much formal education. His "world" was very much that described in a recent book by Lewis O. Saum, *The Popular Mood of Pre–Civil War America*. After studying thousands of letters and private writings of common folk during the period 1800–1860, Saum concluded that an "immense separation [exists] between the modern American and his pre–Civil War ancestor."[5]

That earlier American was much more at home with the culture of Puritanism than the culture of narcissism. The common people Saum described were deeply religious, believing without question in God and the unseen world. Yet they were not much troubled about formal doctrines, ecclesiastical affairs, or the glorious prospect of the millennium, which then preoccupied America's religious elite. Rather, the common people struggled to accept their fate, to overcome guilt, to enjoy the fleeting comforts of love and family, to survive the uncertainties of birth, to eke out existence on an often brutal frontier, and to come to terms with the ever present reality of death. This was the backdrop of Lincoln's religion. It had nothing to do with modern ideas about "finding oneself" or about "God's wonderful plan" for life.

The second circumstance was Lincoln's personal experience with denominational representatives in the Indiana and Illinois of his childhood. In a word, he found the harsh infighting among Methodists, Baptists, Presbyterians, Disciples, Universalists, and "village atheists" repulsive. As a consequence, Lincoln several times professed willingness to join a church that required nothing of its members but heartfelt love to God and to one's neighbors. The competing creeds of the churches were not for him.

The third circumstance was instruction in reality by the coldest master, death. The death of his mother when he was nine, the death of his sister shortly after her marriage, the death of two of his sons (in 1850, and at the White House in 1862), the death of several close friends in the early days of the Civil War (*his* Civil War), and increasingly, the heart-wrenching lists of casualties from the battlefields left him no taste for easy belief, no escape from the mysteries of God and the universe.

The truly remarkable thing about Lincoln's religion was how these circumstances drove him to deeper contemplation of God and the divine will. The external Lincoln, casual about religious observance, hid a man of profound morality and an almost unbearable God consciousness that bound a vision for the nation with the providence of God. This religion, the real faith of Abraham Lincoln, was made up of a nonsectarian attachment to the Scriptures, a growing commitment to prayer, and an unswerving moral consciousness. It also was tied closely to his belief that American ideals reflected the principles of divine morality. These were the beliefs that constructed the paradox of his faith.

THE BIBLE

Although details are scanty about his early study, Lincoln somewhere and somehow acquired a wide and deep knowledge of the Scriptures. In his great debates with Stephen Douglas in 1858, he several times corrected his opponent's inaccurate use of the Bible. After early doubts about the veracity of the Scriptures, he became convinced that they contained the voice of God. In a well-attested story from the last year of his life, Lincoln told an old friend who called himself a skeptic, "Take all this book upon reason that you can, and the balance on faith, and you will live and die a happier and better man."[6]

In that same year he accepted a magnificent ceremonial Bible from "the Loyal Colored People of Baltimore" and replied with oft-quoted words, "In regard to this Great Book, I have but to say, it is the best gift God has given to man. All the good the Saviour gave to the world was communicated through this book. But for it we could not know right from wrong. All things most desirable for man's welfare, here and hereafter, are to be found portrayed in it."[7] In the course of his life, the bare denial of 1846—"I have never denied the truth of the Scriptures"—became something much more positive.

PRAYER

Lincoln, like his political heroes Washington and Jefferson, was intensely private about his religious practice. But it does seem clear that he came to pray more regularly and devoutly as he moved through life. In the middle of the war, he wrote to two Iowans who had commended him for the recent Emancipation Proclamation and assured him of their prayers. In response, Lincoln said he was "sustained by the good wishes and prayers of God's people" in such difficulties.[8] And he often spoke of his own appeals to God for a speedy, just end to the conflict.

As was his habit, Lincoln joked about matters that were most important to him. On more than one occasion he told the story of two Quaker women discussing the war. "I think," said the first, "Jefferson Davis will succeed."

The second asked, "Why does thee think so?"

The reply came, "Because Jefferson is a praying man."

"And so is Abraham a praying man," was the immediate rejoinder.

"Yes," said the first, "but the Lord will think Abraham is joking."[9]

MORAL VISION

Lincoln's personal integrity was undeviating throughout his adult life. Legendary accounts of how as a youth he would expend vast energy to redress trivial discrepancies over pennies or borrowed books

are not required to perceive a person of steady and unswerving morality. And nowhere does his public integrity appear more clearly than
in his opposition to slavery.

Far too many learned books have discussed this issue to give more
than the briefest summary here. But it seems clear that Lincoln was
motivated in his struggle first by his feeling that slavery violated
American principles of freedom. Later on he also came to be more and
more convinced of the rights of all people—even blacks—under God
and under the law.

Lincoln was never a modern egalitarian, and he clung for a long
time to the idea that liberated slaves could be resettled in Africa.
Moreover, he timed the emancipation of the slaves in rebellious states
for maximum political advantage. Yet he also held with growing
conviction that God had called him to national leadership precisely to
extend freedom to all who lived in America, whether they had been
traditionally granted the rights of citizenship or not. Contemporary
advocates of abolition, like the ex-slave statesman Frederick Douglass,
recognized the integrity of Lincoln's actions. After emancipation was
proclaimed on January 1, 1863, for slaves in occupied territory, Douglass, who had earlier criticized the president's delays, wrote in his
journal, "We shout for joy that we live to record this righteous
decree."[10] Lincoln did not posture when he invoked "the considerate
judgment of mankind and the gracious favor of Almighty God" in the
last words of the Proclamation.

LINCOLN'S EVOLVING POLITICAL RELIGION

Much of Lincoln's refined moral sensibility grew out of his love for
American ideals. As a youth he had read Parson Mason Weems's
laudatory biography of George Washington and many other inspiring
accounts of the nation's founding. To Lincoln the ideals of the country,
rather than the political compromises that had been necessary to launch
the government, became beacon lights for his own efforts. He could
call his country "the almost chosen people" and speak of the United
States as "the last, best hope of earth." Such trust respresented a civil
religion, but not of a conventional sort. As the modern religious

historian Martin Marty has put it, Lincoln exercised a "prophetic" style of civil religion.[11] It did not simply assume the nation or its actions had God's blessing, but, rather, felt that the founding ideals had given the country a uniquely moral vision. This was a vision, moreover, that could condemn national immoralities, not just sanction national complacency.

There can be no evading the fact, however, that this was a civil religion, and that it was similar to the political religion responsible for many great wrongs in American history. The reasons that Lincoln's civil religion did not lead to such unfortunate ends are instructive.

Into his presidency, Lincoln was prone to use the words and categories of religion as a way of heightening the dignity of the nation. Thus, in debate with Stephen Douglas (July 10, 1858) Lincoln could use the text, "As your Father in Heaven is perfect, be ye also perfect," to illustrate a seemingly more basic reality: that the laws of the nation should strive to reflect the perfect truth concerning the equality of all men set forth in the Declaration of Independence.[12]

In his first inaugural address of 1861, Lincoln seemed once again to make divine realities the servant of the nation and its destiny. Great was his confidence in the American people: "Why should there not be a patient confidence in the ultimate justice of the people? Is there any better, or equal, hope in the world?" It even seemed as if God existed to harken to the people: "If the Almighty Ruler of nations, with his eternal truth and justice, be on your side of the North, or on yours of the South, that truth, and that justice, will surely prevail, by the judgment of this great tribunal, the American people." The solution in that dark hour was civil religion pure and simple: "Intelligence, patriotism, Christianity, and a firm reliance on Him, who has never yet forsaken this favored land, are still competent to adjust, in the best way, all our present difficulty."[13]

Such a commitment to the godliness of America was deeply ingrained, and it continued during the Civil War. In early 1863, Lincoln was asked to speak at a special meeting of the U. S. Christian Commission, an agency that offered religious and practical assistance to Northern soldiers. Pressing duties prevented Lincoln from accepting the invitation, but he commended the meeting and was also pleased to note the way in which even the calendar was cooperating to drive home the interconnections between God's way and the American way. "The birth-day of Washington, and the Christian Sabbath, coinciding this year, and suggesting together, the highest interests of this life, and of that to come, is most propitious for the meeting proposed."[14]

A hint of this same sentiment appeared in Lincoln's famous Proclamation for a National Fast Day in March 1863. Yet a new note was also sounded in this document, which suggested that Lincoln was beginning to see that the designs of God could not always be tamed for the service of the nation. The proclamation resembled one of the great jeremiads of the Puritans. "It is the duty of nations as well as of men," it began "to own their dependence upon the overruling power of God, to confess their sins and transgressions, in humble sorrow, yet with assured hope that genuine repentance will lead to mercy and pardon." In the hour of need, Americans should remember the blessings they had received and repent of their sin. His words could have been taken from the fast day sermons in seventeenth-century New England: "We have been the recipients of the choicest bounties of Heaven. We have been preserved, these many years, in peace and prosperity. We have grown in numbers, wealth and power, as no other nation has ever grown. But we have forgotten God. . . . Intoxicated with unbroken success, we have become too self-sufficient to feel the necessity of redeeming and preserving grace, too proud to pray to the God that made us!"

In that proclamation, the realities of sin and grace had begun to replace heady confidence in the American people. But the purpose of the proclamation was still largely utilitarian. The practice of good religion would lead to a good political end. And so he concluded: "All this being done, in sincerity and truth, let us then rest humbly in the hope authorized by the Divine teachings, that the united cry of the Nation will be heard on high, and answered with blessings, no less than the pardon of our national sins, and the restoration of our now divided and suffering Country, to its former happy condition of unity and peace."[15] The great war had sobered the rail-splitter from Illinois, but still it was difficult to think that Americans could not move God to do *their* will by the exertion of *their* own great energy.

As early as 1862, however, another note had come to the fore in Lincoln's consciousness. It was the idea that perhaps the will of God could not simply be identified with American ideals and the effort to preserve the American union. He committed such thoughts to paper as early as September 1862, at one of the darkest moments of the war. The Union forces had suffered another disastrous reversal at the Second Battle of Bull Run, and Lincoln was pondering with fresh intensity the radical step of proclaiming the emancipation of slaves in the South. At that time he penned the following "Meditation on the Divine Will," written as his secretaries, Nicolay and Hay, said, "while his mind was burdened with the weightiest questions of his life. . . . It was not written to be seen of men."[16]

The will of God prevails. In great contests each party claims to act in accordance with the will of God. Both *may* be, and one *must* be wrong. God can not be *for,* and *against* the same thing at the same time. In the present civil war it is quite possible that God's purpose is something different from the purpose of either party—and yet the human instrumentalities, working just as they do, are of the best adaptation to effect His purpose. I am almost ready to say this is probably true—that God wills this contest, and wills that it shall not end yet. By his mere quiet power, on the minds of the now contestants, He could have either *saved* or *destroyed* the Union without a human contest. Yet the contest began. And having begun He could give the final victory to either side any day. Yet the contest proceeds.[17]

Like a figure from Israel's ancient history, Lincoln was arguing with God. And it was no longer a domesticated deity, an American God, but the ruler of the nations, who held Lincoln's attention. The truth had begun to dawn that God was not at the nation's beck and call, but the nation at his.

The wrestling that led to this meditation in 1862 seems never to have stopped thereafter. Even as the military tide began to turn in favor of the North, Lincoln continued to sense that the purposes of God could no longer be simply equated with the national purpose. God might be granting the victory to the armies of Grant, Sherman, and Sheridan, but it was no longer simply America's domesticated deity who was bringing this about. The new transcendence in Lincoln's faith, the conviction that the divine concerns went beyond the fortunes of America, came to fullest expression in the eloquent simplicity of his second inaugural address in 1865.

It is no exaggeration to say that there is nothing like this address in the long, often tedious, and frequently hypocritical history of American political discourse. Lincoln briefly reviewed the circumstances that led to the conflict: "Both parties deprecated war; but one of them would *make* war rather than let the nation survive; and the other would *accept* war rather than let it perish." He then singled out division over the extension of slavery as the spark that began a conflict that had lasted far longer than either side expected.

Everything common in American politics, at least in living memory, would lead us to expect that at this point in the speech Lincoln would begin to denounce the South (his foreign enemy) and also defend his policies against opponents in the North. Now was the time to defend his own actions and the actions of his party. Now was the moment for self-justification. Now the moment in the speech had arrived to show the people how wise they had been in returning him to office and how much the future of the country depended upon their nobility. But what came instead was utterly different. The last half of this short address, complete with quotations from Matthew 18:7 and Psalm 19:9, deserves to be quoted in full:

Neither [side] anticipated that the *cause* of the conflict [i.e., slavery] might cease with, or even before, the conflict itself should cease. Each looked for an easier triumph, and a result less fundamental and astounding. Both read the same Bible, and pray to the same God; and each invokes His aid against the other. It may seem strange that any men should dare to ask a just God's assistance in wringing their bread from the sweat of other men's faces; but let us judge not that we be not judged. The prayers of both could not be answered; that of neither has been answered fully. The Almighty has His own purposes. "Woe unto the world because of offences! for it must needs be that offences come; but woe to that man by whom the offence cometh!" If we shall suppose that American Slavery is one of those offences which, in the providence of God, must needs come, but which, having continued through His appointed time, He now wills to remove, and that He gives to both North and South, this terrible war, as the woe due to those by whom the offence came, shall we discern therein any departure from those divine attributes which the believers in a Living God always ascribe to Him? Fondly do we hope—fervently do we pray—that this mighty scourge of war may speedily pass away. Yet, if God wills that it continue, until all the wealth piled by the bond-man's two hundred and fifty years of unrequited toil shall be sunk, and until every drop of blood drawn with the lash, shall be paid by another drawn with the sword, as was said three thousand years ago, so still it must be said "the judgments of the Lord, are true and righteous altogether."

With malice toward none; with charity for all; with firmness in the right, as God gives us to see the right, let us strive on to finish the work we are in; to bind up the nation's wounds; to care for him who shall have borne the battle, and for his widow, and his orphan—to do all which may achieve and cherish a just, and a lasting peace, among ourselves, and with all nations.[18]

Five weeks after he delivered this address on March 4, 1865, Lincoln was dead—and American politics returned to "normal." What was missing immediately thereafter, and what has been largely missing since, is Lincoln's unique blend of convictions:

—that the nation embodies lofty ideals about human dignity and worth;
—that these ideals are an expression of truths grounded in the Scriptures of the New, but especially of the Old Testament;
—that these ideals show us how far short we fall in most of our national life;
—that God's judgment falls rightfully upon all of us, for personal and national sins alike;
—that national trauma is regularly deserved for the way in which we, as citizens, sanction or tolerate abuses against humanity;
—and that in spite of our weakness and guilt, God's providence rules over the affairs of people and nations.

No one before or after Lincoln said such things so clearly. We have heard many leaders in politics and religion champion the ideals of the nation, but rarely with Lincoln's clear sense that no party, no self-appointed guardians of public morality, no narrowly factional interest group, can embody the national ideals. We have had many call the nation to repentence, but few with the conviction that all stand guilty before God—even those who issue the call. We have had many who equate the United States with transcendent good, and more recently many who have identified it with root evil. But we have had precious few who, with Lincoln, have perceived how thoroughly the good and evil intermingle in our heritage, how completely our hope for the public future runs up against the legacies of private and corporate wrong.

In the end it is an irony that Lincoln, the man of deep, but unconventional faith, has so much to teach Christians of a more conventional faith. A harsh upbringing, a melancholy disposition, a profound understanding of those Scriptures that portray the overarching providence of God, and an existential awareness of life's transitory character gave Lincoln a grasp on reality that few of us ever achieve.

PARADOX AND TRANSCENDENCE

The paradox of Lincoln's faith once again resembles the paradoxical character of faith in New England Puritanism. Like the Puritans, Lincoln possessed a deeply rooted belief in the sovereign Lord of the Scriptures, especially as revealed in the mysterious ways of Jehovah with the Hebrews. Like the Puritans, however, he also believed that God had chosen America to be the scene of his further manifestation to the world. Lincoln went beyond the Puritans to locate that manifestation in human documents, the Declaration of Independence and the Constitution. And that establishes the paradox: this compound faith inspired Lincoln, as it had the Puritans, to public actions of a profoundly Christian character. It moved him, as it had moved them, to the clearest perception in our history of the moral dimensions of public life. Lincoln and the Puritans were wrong about America being a unique manifestation of God's presence. Yet if they had not believed in the divinity of America, they would not have exerted such efforts at structuring public life according to the biblical will of God.

These reflections lead naturally to the question, Were the Puritans and Lincoln in fact so wrong about America? Might not their dedication lead us to take more seriously the strong God-and-America assumption? But this will not do. The great good that such convictions have led to have been counterbalanced by great evil from the same source. The civil religion, which in Lincoln led to good, has propelled many others to acts of great evil. However strong the consciousness in America of extraordinary divine blessing, the "people of God" are those who trust him in all times and all parts of the world. Samuel Hopkins, the student of Jonathan Edwards and an antislavery activist during the Revolutionary period, was surely correct when he wrote in 1776, "the distinction [of Israel] is . . . at an end, and all nations are put upon a level; and Christ . . . has taught us to look on all nations as our neighbors and brethren."[19]

Surely Lincoln overestimated both the eternal value of American ideals and the godly potential of the American people. But just as surely *his* civil religion resulted in greater good for the nation than the activities of many who have abandoned the idea of America's uniqueness under God.

In the end, the good that came out of Lincoln's political faith may have had more to do with his religion than his politics. This was a religion that, even as it spoke to Lincoln in his American circumstances, called him to acknowledge God's mysterious sovereignty over all nations.

Lincoln knew he was no saint. "I have often wished that I was a more devout man than I am," he told a delegation of Baltimore Presbyterians in 1863. Yet this ability to see himself realistically—to acknowledge that he had no right to condemn the unjust as if he had never sinned—allowed him to glimpse the realistic potential of human dignity. Even more, it allowed him to recognize that above and beyond all nations and national ideals, God prevailed. "Amid the greatest difficulties of my Administration," he went on to his visitors from Baltimore, "when I could not see any other resort, I would place my whole reliance in God, knowing that all would go well, and that He would decide for the right."[20]

Lincoln had no illusions about what it meant for "all" to "go well." Whatever the deficiencies in his personal faith or religious practice, he knew, at the most profound level, where the world, the nation, and his own destiny fit into the scheme of things. A humorous statement that we have already cited makes this point so well that it bears repetition. During the war he told visitors who prayed for God to be on "their" side that he was much more concerned that *they* be on God's side. Lincoln was not a conventional Christian, but this president of humor and inner torment, this ordinary extraordinary man, had nonetheless begun to render to God the things that are God's.

7. The Promise and Peril of Reform I: Abolition

No aspect of American history reveals more of the complexity of the relationship between God and Caesar than the Christian drive for social reform. An unending series of efforts to mold society after general Christian principles or specific biblical injunctions stretches from the beginning of European colonization to the present. These efforts have been directed toward a multitude of goals, from causes that have won the favorable judgment of history (like the attack on slavery) to those that now appear quixotic (like the nineteenth-century campaign against Masonry), from matters that now are taken for granted (like the movement to provide humane care for the mentally ill) to those that remain controversial (like the current battle over abortion on demand). Many of these movements have led to the rehabilitation of individuals and the significant improvement of American life. Some have been spectacular failures. Almost all have been in some sense ironic; that is, they have brought changes in society, or changes in the reformers themselves, that were not anticipated when the reform got under way. Almost all have also had some effect, whether anticipated or not, on the religion practiced by the reformers.

This chapter and the next contain brief accounts of two of the most significant efforts of Christian reform in our history, abolition (the drive against slavery) and prohibition (the campaign against the consumption of beverage alcohol). These two movements for reform were the most dynamic such efforts of the nineteenth century, when Christian values exerted their greatest influence on American society. They were important not only because of the reforms themselves but also because of wider religious and political issues. They are also significant because they show clearly what Christian political action has been able to accomplish in American society, what it has not been able to do, and how such action affects the Christian faith itself.

After examining the outworking of these two reform movements, we will be in a better position to analyze several important features of Christian political behavior in America. As has so often been characteristic of American reform movements, both were connected to the rise of revivalism, and both shared the virtues and vices of revival. They both also shared the strong drive for perfection that characterized the nineteenth-century revivals and, therefore, illustrate the strengths and weaknesses of Christian political action based on a perfectionist model. Finally, both show the importance of the Bible for movements of Christian social reform. In so doing they reveal how powerfully the Scriptures speak to the realities of day-to-day social life, but also how tempting it is to subordinate the message of the Bible to the compelling needs of a specific movement for reform.

ABOLITION AS A CHRISTIAN CAUSE

The attack on slavery as a social institution had both Christian and more general origins. In the late seventeenth century and on into the eighteenth century, individuals and a few organized groups began to speak out against chattel bondage, especially as practiced on Africans. Some did so for humanitarian reasons or because they saw an inconsistency between slavery and newer ideas of personal liberty. Others, like the Quakers and some Mennonites, began to protest against slavery because of its intrinsic violation of Christian values.

In America a weighty, if never overwhelming, antislavery stance emerged out of the colonial revival known as the Great Awakening. This renewal of evangelical Calvinism, which peaked during the 1740s, laid special emphasis on the equality of all before God and the freedom of God's sovereign grace. One of its by-products was a fresh effort to evangelize enslaved blacks and to improve their worldly condition. Leaders of the Awakening like England's George Whitefield or Samuel Davies, the foremost revivalist in Virginia, did not attack slaveholding itself, but they did go much further than their peers in the English-speaking Protestant churches to treat slaves as human beings and to attack white assaults upon black dignity.

EVANGELICAL ANTISLAVERY AFTER THE REVOLUTION

From their work emerged a more direct Christian assault upon slavery at the end of the century.[1] The more general American concern for liberty, which was nurtured by the struggle for independence from Britain, contributed to this antislavery effort. From the Revolution the reformers took the conviction that white enslavement of blacks was as bad as "slavery" to Parliament's power of taxation.

The legacy from the colonial revival loomed just as large. That Christian heritage provided evangelical reformers with several weapons for the attack on slavery. As children of the Great Awakening, they stressed the transforming power of conversion; they praised the virtues of activistic Christianity; they raised the possibility that the millennium (a thousand-year reign of Christ on the earth) might lie at the end of their efforts; they affirmed the desirability of suffering for the cause of Christ; and they held out an apostolic ideal of simple daily life. With such convictions, leaders in several denominations set out after the Revolution to wipe the evil of slavery from the land. They included Methodists (Francis Asbury, Freeborn Garrettson, William McKendree), Presbyterians (Jacob Green, David Rice), Congregationalists (Samuel Hopkins, Levi Hart), and representatives of several other denominations. Their general feeling was that if they could show the imcompatibility between slavery and principles of both Christianity and the Revolution, individual slaveholders would see the error of their ways and agree to free their slaves.

This Christian antislavery activity was augmented by the support of more secular humanitarians. Thomas Jefferson, for instance, though he was a slaveholder himself, held that the institution was harmful and should be abolished after a suitable period of preparation for both masters and slaves. For a very few years it seemed as if the combination of Christian pressure and more general dissatisfaction with slavery would end the "peculiar institution" in the wake of the Revolutionary War.

But then a number of factors came into play to quench that impulse. Changing national conditions, especially the beginning of a Southern political consciousness and the growing profitability of cotton as an export crop, hamstrung the cause. In the North, the states gradually provided for the manumission of slaves, which led to a relaxation of abolitionist sentiment there. In the South, where abolitionism had been reasonably strong after the War, there was less and less interest in freedom for blacks.

Christian efforts also began to flag during the 1790s and beyond. As we have seen when considering the election campaign of 1800, Protestant evangelicals in the North, who had spearheaded the earlier effort against slavery, became increasingly disenchanted with political action. These evangelicals devoted their energies more and more to other causes, like foreign missions, revivals, and the alleged threat to society from "infidel" conspiracies. When, therefore, Congress exercised its constitutional prerogative in 1808 to ban the importation of slaves, most Christians assumed that the most important goal had been achieved. Some moved on immediately to other reforms. For others, a rise in social status brought increased contact and friendship with slaveholders. Still others actually emigrated from slave to free states. The combination of these factors defused most of the Christian abolitionist concern that survived into the nineteenth century.

The most important antislavery movement in the next twenty years was the American Colonization Society, founded in 1816 with the intent of sending liberated slaves back to Africa. Its organizers hoped that this venture would address an American evil at the same time that it made possible the evangelization of Africa by Christian blacks. The leaders of this society were a diverse, even contradictory group. Some, like the noted Presbyterian evangelist and educator Samuel Finley, pursued antislavery activity from religious motives. But others actually favored slavery and looked upon the Society as a way of ridding the country of free blacks. The fact that America's blacks themselves were never enthusiastic about this project did not stop it from becoming the best-known antislavery vehicle into the 1830s.

REVIVALISTIC ABOLITIONISM

The spread of revivalism was the occasion for a great renewal of antislavery activity in the late 1820s and into the 1830s. There had been fresh outbursts of revival in New England from the early 1790s and on the western frontier (mostly Kentucky and Tennessee) from the early 1800s. Their number and intensity continued to grow throughout the early decades of the century. In the South these stirrings of revival led to an increasing Christianization of the population and a growing acceptance of the Christian faith in the upper, or planter, class, a group that at best was only nominally Christian until the nineteenth century. In the North revival brought a growing body of adherents to the churches, especially the rapidly growing Methodist and Baptist churches. It also led to more determined efforts at righting social as well as individual wrongs.

THE QUALITIES OF REVIVALISM

Revivalism in the 1820s and 1830s was fueled by many dramatic leaders, of whom Charles Grandison Finney (1792–1875) was the most important.[2] Finney was converted in 1821 while preparing for a career as a lawyer. Immediately he gave up the law and began to preach, because, as he testified, he had received "a retainer from the Lord." Soon his forceful and logical message of divine forgiveness and human holiness, combined with a dynamic personality of great charisma, catapulted him into national leadership. Finney was an innovator, both in theology (where he placed increasing stress on the ability of individuals to call upon God and to lead holy lives) and in revivalistic practice (where he pioneered with "protracted" meetings, held nightly for an extended period in one locality, and with the "anxious bench," a special area set aside for sinners under conversion to pray through to their salvation). Finney's revivalism was important not only in the general history of American religion, but also more specifically to the development of Christian political action, for the style of his revivals became the dominant form of Christian public behavior in his day and since. In a word, Finney was an "immediatist," an "ultraist," and a "perfectionist."

Finney's watchward was salvation now. As one of his colleagues put it in describing an early campaign, the revivalist urged "sinners to repent and submit to Jesus Christ, and that *immediately,* as the only condition of forgiveness."[3] For our purposes, it is important to note that Finney thought of daily life, as well as of conversion, in immediate terms. Now that they were Christians, converts had both the ability and the duty to reform every aspect of their lives, and to do so immediately.

Finney, the immediatist, was also an "ultraist," a phrase used as early as 1835 to describe the revivals in Finney's upstate New York, a region known as "the Burned-over District" for the parade of religious enthusiasms that swept over it in the first half of the nineteenth century.[4] Finney held that where individuals could see the path to truth and righteousness, they must set aside all else in order to pursue it. And they were responsible for pursuing it *now*. Any delay in following the commands of God—to repent of sin, to cleanse one's life, to pursue holiness—was itself a sin.

Finney was important for his age, not so much because he succeeded in getting others to follow him (though he had a wide and loyal following), but because he so embodied the aggressive, confident spirit of American Christianity before the Civil War. "Revivalism," as one historian of American reform before the Civil War has written, "was the core of antebellum Protestantism."[5] It was an age of national advance geographically (to the Mississippi and beyond). It was an age of heady democratic rhetoric (the heyday of Andrew Jackson and "the common man"). It was an age of abundance, or at least of economic opportunity for all, immigrant or long-time resident, who could work hard to take advantage of opportunities. And it was an age of Christian action. No evil, personal or social, seemed strong enough to withstand the revivalist's word. No task, in the reform of the self or the reform of the world, was too daunting for the Christian inspired by a sense of divine calling. If only believers would devote their energies to the cause, if only they would enlist under the banner of Christ, then the local community, the nation, and even the world lay open before them to be won for the kingdom of God.

As revival and reform captured the imagination of American Christians, the conviction grew stronger that a perfect state of society could be achieved. "Perfection" was a goal that could, it seemed, be reached. With God's help and a steady exertion of will, personal and social evils could be overcome, and a better way of life, perhaps even the long-anticipated millennium, would emerge. One man who expressed this belief forcefully was John Humphrey Noyes, a Vermonter who experienced a revivalistic conversion as a young man and who was inspired by Christian ideals taught at evangelical institutions of higher education (Dartmouth, Andover Seminary, Yale Divinity School) and by colleagues of Charles Finney. In the 1840s Noyes eventually founded his own separated, communitarian villages, first at Putney, Vermont, and then at Oneida, New York. He did so because he felt the burdens of normal society were retarding the attainment of perfection, a goal to be sought at all costs. Noyes put it like this: "As the doctrine of temperance is total abstinence from alcoholic drinks, and the doctrine of antislavery is immediate abolition of human bondage, so the doctrine of perfectionism is the immediate and total cessation from sin."[6] At least in Noyes's mind, this perfectionism was a logical outgrowth of the kind of revival promoted by Charles Finney; as he saw it, it led naturally to the sort of reform efforts exemplified by abolitionism. Most Protestants did not go as far as Noyes, but many did come to believe that, with God's help, it was possible to approach perfection in this life.

FROM REVIVALISM TO ABOLITIONISM: CHARLES G. FINNEY

The ultraism, immediatism, and perfectionism of revivalism greatly stimulated Christian activity, both in politics and in other arenas. By 1820, America's Protestants had formed separate organizations for the promotion of missionary work at home and abroad, for the distribution of Bibles, and for returning freed slaves to Africa. In the 1820s came the American Society for the Promotion of Temperance, the American Tract Society, and the American Education Society (which helped thousands of young men prepare for the ministry). Soon there followed a wealth of movements promoting manual labor, anti-Masonry, dietary reform, seamen's benevolence, women's rights, aid to the mentally ill, hypnotism, prison reform, sanitary hospital care, rehabilitation for prostitutes, Sunday schools for working children, the water cure, industrial reform, phrenology, and many other causes—all in the interest of conquering the world for Christ. Some of the new voluntary societies were immediately successful; some found the going much more difficult. The most comprehensive reform proved to be the hardest: it was the effort to abolish slavery.

From the mid-1820s, a growing number of converts in the revival, who came naturally to add social concern to evangelistic purposes, turned their attention to the institution of slavery. Charles Finney himself early took a strong stand against slavery, and some of his converts went even further to campaign for its abolition. Finney did not want the fight against slavery to replace "the main question of saving souls," but he left no doubts about his convictions concerning slavery. As he put it in his *Lectures on Revivals of Religion* of 1835:

The subject of Slavery is a subject upon which Christians, praying men, *need not* and *must not* differ. . . . Christians can no more take neutral ground on this subject, since it has come up for discussion, than they can take neutral ground on the subject of the sanctification of the Sabbath. It is a great national sin. It is a sin of the church. The churches, by their silence, and by permitting slaveholders to belong to their communion, have been consenting to it. All denominations have been more or less guilty. . . . I believe the time has come, and although I am no prophet, I believe it will be found to have come, that the revival in the United States will continue and prevail, no farther and faster than the church take right ground upon this subject. . . . It is the church that mainly supports this sin. Her united testimony upon the subject would settle the question. Let Christians of all denominations meekly, but firmly, come forth, and pronounce their verdict; let them wash their hands of this thing; let them give forth and write on the head and front of this great abomination, SIN, and in three years, a public sentiment would be formed that would carry all before it, and there would not be a shackled slave, nor a bristling, cruel slavedriver in this land.[7]

Sentiments like Finney's dominated Christian antislavery activity in the 1830s. The emphasis was on the effort to convert individuals to Christianity and then to convince converted Christians that slavery was a moral evil to be repudiated. As a child of his age, Finney was confident that the message was clear, that he and similarly gifted revivalists could get it through, and that (once understood) the word about the evil of slavery would lead to its immediate repeal. In the first years of revived antislavery activity, direct political action was not in the picture. Political improvement would come indirectly. The converted sinner, the redeemed heart, would bring an end to this evil.

REVIVALISTIC ABOLITIONISTS: WELD, GARRISON, LOVEJOY

The abolitionist drive of the 1830s enlisted many dynamic Christian leaders, some directly associated with Finney's revivals in New York, others drawn from the evangelical culture of New England. Chief among the former was the spellbinding speaker and indefatigable organizer Theodore Dwight Weld (1803–1895).[8] Weld was converted in 1826 during Finney's great revival campaign in Utica, New York. He soon became an ardent advocate of reform, lending his skills first to the promotion of universal manual labor as the solution to problems of poverty, worker exploitation, and greed. Later he would also become a promoter of the rights of women. But the heart of his reforming interest was always abolition.

Weld's most notable early success in that effort came in 1834 at Lane Theological Seminary in Cincinnati, a Presbyterian school financed both by local churches and by reformers from New York and New England. In the spring of that year Weld conducted what might be called today a "teach-in," eighteen days filled with prayer meetings, lengthy discussions of the slavery problem, and fiery lectures each evening. It was the model of Finney's revivals applied to social reform. Weld soon won over almost the entire student body to the support of immediate abolition. When the local trustees—cautious ministers and businessmen very much aware of the proslavery sentiment just across the Ohio River in Kentucky (a slave state) and in Cincinnati itself— attempted to restrain the young reformers, Weld and most of his supporters left the institution. Soon they found a new home in Oberlin, Ohio, where they helped transform a struggling local institution into Oberlin College. That school in turn became a center of both evangelical revivalism (Charles Finney came as the professor of theology in 1835) and Christian social action (Oberlin was an important stop on the "underground railroad" transporting escaped slaves to Canada, and it was also the nation's first college to admit women students on the same basis as men).

For the next decade, Weld stood at the forefront of the nation's abolitionists. He traveled tirelessly to small communities preaching the message of immediate release for the slaves. In the early 1840s he spearheaded the move that pushed the issue of slavery into the halls of Congress in Washington, D.C., where he mobilized support and provided staff service for abolitionist congressmen. For Weld, abolition was the great crusade: In his words, it "not only *overshadows* all others, but . . . absorbs them into itself. Revivals, moral Reform etc. will remain stationary until the temple is cleansed."[9]

Even more important as a symbol of the all-out war against slavery was William Lloyd Garrison (1805–1879), an accomplished publicist raised in New England and dedicated to idealistic Christian goals. Garrison's early religious instruction came from Quakers and so did not exactly parallel the revivalistic experiences of Finney and Weld. But he was every bit as much a religious opponent of the slave system and just as determined to reach a perfect state of society. In 1828 he set out his life's calling in an editorial for the prohibitionist newspaper he was then editing:

While there remains a tyrant to sway the iron rod of power, or chain about the body or mind to be broken, I cannot surrender my arms. While drunkenness and intemperance abound, I will try to reclaim the dissolute, and to annihilate the progress of vice. While profanity and sabbath-breaking, and crime wound my ear and affect my sight, I will reprove, admonish and condemn. While the demon of war is urging mankind to deeds of violence and revenge, I will "study the things that make for peace." While a soul remains unenlightened, uneducated, and without "the glorious gospel of the blessed God," my duty is plain—I will contribute my little influence to the diffusion of universal knowledge.[10]

To reach his goals, Garrison disdained the give-and-take of politics; he voted only once in his entire life (for Lincoln in 1864). But in disdaining politics, he did not disdain action with political consequences. From his concern for many reforms, Garrison soon concentrated full attention on what he saw as the greatest of American evils, the continuation of slavery.

In time, Garrison became the Finney of abolitionism, the John

Humphrey Noyes of antislavery. The establishment of his newspaper, *The Liberator,* in Boston in 1831 marked a new stage in Christian antislavery activity. Its battle cry was "immediate emancipation" (by which was meant an immediate decision to end slavery, even though the actual process might take a few years). All other solutions to the slave dilemma were suspect, including what Garrison called "the pernicious doctrine of *gradual* abolition."[11] To Garrison, it was obvious that the concentration of moral energy would lead sinners to perceive their error, to repent of their sin, and to free the slaves.

Garrison's zeal in pursuit of this goal knew no bounds. *"I will be as harsh as truth, and as uncompromising as justice,"* he announced in the first issue of *The Liberator.* And he went on:

On this subject, I do not wish to think, or speak, or write, with moderation. No! no! Tell a man whose house is on fire to give a moderate alarm; tell him to moderately rescue his wife from the hands of a ravisher; tell the mother to gradually extricate her babe from the fire into which it has fallen;—but urge me not to use moderation in a cause like the present. I am in earnest—I will not equivocate—I will not excuse—I will not retreat a single inch— AND I WILL BE HEARD.[12]

The abolitionist movement gained a martyr in November 1837 when another fiery publisher, Elijah Lovejoy, was killed by a mob while he defended his printing press in Alton, Illinois. Lovejoy, like many of the abolitionists, was diligent for many reforms. He saw, for instance, the hand of the pope behind the institution of slavery, so he considered a blow against slavery to be also a blow against the Catholic church, which he, along with other revivalists, like Lyman Beecher, thought was the Antichrist. Lovejoy had been driven out of St. Louis by resistance to his abolitionism, but he vowed never to leave his post in Alton, across the Mississippi River. "Should I attempt it," he said shortly before his death in a speech that admirers repeated many times, "I should feel that the angel of the Lord, with his flaming sword, was pursuing me wherever I went. It is because I fear God that I am not afraid of all who oppose me in this city."[13] It was at a memorial service for Lovejoy in Ohio that the thirty-year-old John Brown pledged himself to the lifelong struggle against slavery that would end with his raid on Harper's Ferry in 1859 and his hanging as a martyr to the cause of abolition.

POLITICS AS PERSONAL MORALITY

Throughout the 1830s the battle was waged on the moral terms highlighted by Finney, Weld, Garrison, and Lovejoy. The abolitionist societies in the North, especially the American Anti-Slavery Society, flooded the South with literature calling for repentance and reform. Other intrepid abolitionists spoke and published in the North, where the battle lines were more complicated. Most Northerners were pleased with the absence of slavery in their states, but many in the North, inside and outside the churches, were white supremacists opposed to the settlement of blacks (free or slave) in the opening West. Many distrusted the zealotry of the abolitionists. And some of the supporters of abolition still felt it would be wise to send liberated slaves to Africa. Convictions on slavery were complex, and it was turning out to take longer than the three years envisioned by Charles Finney to bring the system to an end.

One of the reasons for the delay was growing opposition to the abolitionists from other Christians. Southerners were shocked in 1831 when, only months after the founding of Garrison's *Liberator,* a band of slaves in Virginia rose in rebellion under the leadership of Nat Turner. The reaction was swift and frenzied. Southern legislatures passed tougher laws limiting slave activities, the last Southern abolitionists were silenced, and great umbrage was taken at Northern meddling. Even Christian leaders, some of whom were admittedly troubled by the institution, began to express the opinion that slavery was a worldly issue beyond the spiritual concern of the church. By the mid-1830s, Southerners, including Christians, were taking aggressive steps to counteract abolitionist influence. These extended to an interdiction on abolitionist literature mailed from the North. And they included a specific counterattack against the Northern use of the Bible.

SLAVERY AND THE BIBLE

Growing strife over the use of Scripture was, in fact, one of the most notable developments among American churches during the 1830s and 1840s. Northern Christians might differ among themselves as to how abrupt the end of slavery should be or whether slaveholders should be compensated when their slaves were freed. And some prominent denominational leaders joined their Southern colleagues in questioning whether the church should speak out on slavery. But the general sentiment of Northern Christians was that biblical religion and the slave system were incompatible.

Albert Barnes, a Philadelphia Presbyterian minister, expressed this feeling in a book published in 1846, *An Inquiry into the Scriptural Views of Slavery*. Its arguments, or others similar to them, appeared time after time in the work of the Northern Christian abolitionists. In Barnes's words, "The principles laid down by the Saviour and his Apostles are such as are opposed to Slavery, and if carried out would secure its universal abolition."[14] To Barnes, the Bible was both clear and self-evident. Scripture taught the equal dignity of all women and men as human beings made by God; it showed how all had the natural right to be protected in the bond of marriage and to worship God freely. Most importantly, "the gospel, and the Bible generally, prohibits, in the most positive manner, many things which are always found in slavery, and which are inescapable from it"—like man-stealing, "the kind of oppression which always enters into the idea of slavery," and the deprivation of lawful wages. In sum, "the spirit of the Christian religion is against it; . . . the fair application of the Christian religion would remove it from the world, BECAUSE *it is an evil, and is displeasing to God.*"[15]

The response of Southerners, and a few Northern social conservatives, was to accuse Barnes and like-minded writers of twisting the Bible to their own purposes. Did not God's Old Testament people, including Abraham the faithful patriarch, hold slaves? Did not the Apostle Paul send the slave Onesimus back to his master Philemon? And did not the same apostle tell slaves not to seek their freedom if they were called to Christ while in that condition (1 Cor. 7:21)? Responding directly to Albert Barnes, the Reverend Frederick Ross of Huntsville, Alabama, insisted that Southern slavery amounted to a direct parallel to the biblical pattern:

Every Southern planter is not more truly a slaveholder than Abraham. And the Southern master, by divine authority, may today, consider his slaves part of his social and religious family, just as Abraham did. He has slaves of an inferior type of mankind from Abraham's bondmen; and he therefore, for that reason, as well as from the fact that they are his slaves, holds them lower than himself. But, nevertheless, he is a slaveholder in no other sense than was Abraham. . . . So, then, Abraham lived in the midst of a system of slave-holding, exactly the same in nature with that in the South—a system ordained of God as really as the other forms of government round about him.[16]

Other ministers were eager to match texts with abolitionists in defense of the proposition, as a Georgian put it in 1856, "that the system of slavery in the United States, in every feature and in every particular of every feature, is essentially the same as the system authorized by the Bible."[17] When in October 1845 two Presbyterian clergymen in Cincinnati took four days to debate each other on the subject of slavery, the more conservative, N. L. Rice, concluded that what abolitionists were attacking as sin had been authorized by God himself. Only by rejecting the truthfulness of the Bible could abolitionists avoid such a conclusion:

The fact . . . is clearly established, if language can establish it, that God did recognize the relation of master and slave as, under the circumstances, lawful, and did give express permission to the Jews to purchase slaves from the heathen, and hold them. . . . [My opponent] must admit, that God gave the Jews permission, under certain circumstances, to form the relation which he denounces as in itself sinful; or he must deny that the Old Testament is the word of God.[18]

The Bible, it seems, could be a resource on both sides. As the debate continued, it became clearer that abolition would not come about simply by quoting passages from the Book of Acts about God not respecting persons (10:34) or creating all persons from one blood (17:-26). The opponents of the abolitionists also knew how to read and quote the Scriptures.

THE DECLINE OF REVIVALISTIC ABOLITION

During the 1830s, Christian abolitionists succeeded in pushing the moral question of slavery into the forefront of the nation's consciousness. Very often, however, they were not successful in convincing fellow Christians—Southerners caught up in the slave economy but also many Northerners who yet resisted abolition—that their cause was practical, right, or even Christian. And so the Christian crusade against slavery, which began in the wake of revival and as the almost intuitive consequence of revival, started to unravel. Abolitionists more and more began to disagree with each other, even as they worked against the grain of American opinion. Some held that reformers should promote all possible ways of improving American life; others considered energy diverted from the movement against slavery as wasted energy. Some felt that the time for political action had come; others, like William Lloyd Garrison, maintained their distance from electoral politics.

A combination of factors in the late 1830s and early 1840s effectively ended the first phase of revivalistic Christian abolition. Stiffened opposition in the North, from mob violence to reasoned argument, discouraged some reformers. A severe economic collapse in 1837 hit the financial backers of the American Anti-Slavery Society especially hard. And then the country's three largest Protestant denominations—the Presbyterians, the Baptists, and the Methodists—split apart, and so greatly limited the most important channels for circulating exhortations to social reform.[19] The division of the Presbyterians in 1837 had theological as well as social origins and was not a neat North-South split. One of its major causes, however, was a clash over tactics toward slavery. Those who advocated ardent opposition went one way; those who counseled caution or who defended the slave system went the other way. When Baptists and Methodists divided in 1844–1845, slavery was the central issue, and the resulting division left these two growing denominations divided into northern and southern bodies. The issue in both cases was whether the denomination as a whole should give its sponsorship to slaveholders. When the issue could no longer be avoided, Northerners and Southerners went their separate ways with considerable bitterness.

Internal dissension also slowed the abolitionist effort. Differences of opinion on whether the American Anti-Slavery Society should participate directly in political maneuvering and whether it should actively promote greater opportunities for women eventually led to the division of that body in 1840. After this split, abolitionists on both sides of these questions continued to advocate reform, but their voice was weaker for being divided on the other concerns.

THE TURN TO POLITICS

Abolitionist political activity was well under way before the Anti-Slavery Society divided over the issue. One of the first overtly political maneuvers came in the mid-1830s when abolitionists, taking advantage of the guarantee in the First Amendment of the right to petition the national government "for a redress of grievances," inundated Congress with letters containing thousands of signatures. Soon other, more aggressive action followed. In the early 1840s Theodore Dwight Weld led other abolitionists in doing research and preparing speeches for antislavery Whig legislators, including the aged ex-president John Quincy Adams, who from his seat in the House became the doughty champion of political abolitionism. As early as 1835, Charles Finney was insisting that *"The church must take right ground in regard to politics."* Finney did not mean the creation of a Christian political party. He did mean that "the time has come that Christians must vote for honest men, and take consistent ground in politics, or the Lord will curse them. . . . They must let the world see that the church will uphold no man in office, who is known to be a knave, or an adulterer, or a Sabbath-breaker, or a gambler, or a drunkard."[20] Soon Finney and others who shared his revivalistic faith had added "slaveholder" and "supporter of slavery" to the list of sins disqualifying a man for political office. The desire to attack slavery through the conviction of individual consciences did not die out by any means, but a determination to take direct political action became increasingly important as the 1830s gave way to the next decade.

A growing desire among abolitionists for political results led to the formation of a single-issue antislavery party in time for the 1840 presidential elections. The campaign of that year matched the incumbent, Democrat Martin Van Buren, against the Whig challenger, General William Henry Harrison. Van Buren pledged himself to veto any bill passed by Congress to abolish slavery in the District of Columbia; Harrison (himself not an ardent abolitionist) announced his intention to sign whatever laws Congress might chose to pass on the subject. That was enough for some abolitionists, but not enough for those, including a large proportion of Christian activists, who formed the Liberty party, with its platform of immediate abolition. In the event, General Harrison, a hero from the War of 1812, swamped Van Buren, whose fate was sealed by adverse reaction to the economic collapse of 1837. Neither did the Liberty party fare well, receiving only 6,000 votes nationwide. But when General Harrison died one month after taking office in 1841, the abolitionists of the Liberty party had cause to berate their fellows who had gone with Harrison. The vice president who succeeded Harrison was John Tyler of Virginia, a slaveholder, who though a Whig, surrounded himself with Southern advisers and refused to countenance any restriction of slavery.

This turn in national affairs gave added zeal to the leaders of the Liberty party, who felt that nothing but fervent dedication to abolition would restore the tarnished moral character of the nation.[21] As the election of 1844 approached, the activists of the Liberty party were encouraged. They had garnered 65,000 votes in state elections (in the North) in 1843, and they had even succeeded in beginning a branch of their national organization in Virginia. Their candidate in 1844, as also four years earlier, was James G. Birney, a former slaveholder from Alabama, whose double conversion (to evangelical Protestantism and to abolition) had been one of the most encouraging developments for antislavery activists in the early 1830s. The Democrats, divided between supporters of Martin Van Buren and John C. Calhoun, put up James K. Polk of Tennessee as a compromise choice. For Southern Democrats, and many Northern ones as well, the key issue in the campaign was the admission of Texas as a slave state. The Whig choice was Henry Clay, the much-respected "Great Compromiser" from Kentucky who had worked in the Congress for over thirty years to defuse sectional antagonisms and restrict the spread of slavery. Clay's moderation was too much for ardent Christian abolitionists who thought they could see an opening for Birney and the Liberty party, if not to win the 1844 election, at least to set up a great national triumph in 1848.

In the end, the supporters of the Liberty party succeeded only in giving the country the most thoroughly slave-supporting administration in its history. Birney did do considerably better than in 1840, with 62,000 popular votes (slightly over 2 percent of the approximately 2,700,000 recorded that year). But the vote for Birney in Michigan and New York, votes that normally would have gone to Clay and the Whigs as the superior alternative on slavery, kept Clay from winning those states and gave the election to Polk. In his turn, President Polk filled the cabinet with slaveholders and embarked on an aggressive policy of strengthening laws protecting slavery in the South and expanding protection of slavery into new western lands.

After 1844, Christian abolitionism was more fragmented. Some reformers once again renounced political activity, and some returned to support the Whig party. Still others continued to press for a new political alignment. Some of the abolitionists dissatisfied with both Whigs and Democrats supported the Free-Soil party in 1848 and 1852, a mixed group resembling to some extent the early Colonization Society. Free-Soilers included abolitionists but also white racists who wanted to keep the West free from blacks altogether. When the new Republican party first ran a presidential candidate in the 1856 election, it too garnered considerable support from Christian abolitionists. Yet from their first entrance onto the national scene, Republicans were always more a "free-soil" party, determined not to let slavery spread into the territories or new states, than an abolitionist party. As we have seen, the successful Republican candidate of 1860, Abraham Lincoln, did not move to emancipate the slaves until 1862, and only then in the Southern states still in rebellion against the Union. Most abolitionists came to respect Lincoln and to work through the Republican party for their goals. But as Free-Soilers or Republicans it was never possible, as it had been in 1840 and 1844 with the Liberty party, to pursue abolition without compromise, delay, and frustration.

From 1840 and the establishment of the Liberty party through the passage of the Civil War amendments to the Constitution from 1865 to 1870 (banning slavery, guaranteeing ex-slaves citizenship and the right to vote), Christian agitation against slavery moved by fits and starts. To be sure, it was deeply embedded in the more general political history of the country, a confused and confusing history that involved the Compromise of 1850, with its harsh Fugitive Slave Law, the

Kansas-Nebraska Act of 1854 that opened up most of the Western territories to the possibility of slavery, the Dred Scott case of 1857 whereby the Supreme Court defined slaves as the absolute property of their masters, the Lincoln–Douglas debates of 1858, and the complicated maneuvering that led to Lincoln's election in 1860, the secession of the Confederate states, and the outbreak of war at Fort Sumter in early 1861. In other words, during the period in which historians trace the development of "political abolitionism," Christians were by no means passive or silent. Yet amidst the tumult of the times, it was hard to hear their voice as clearly as it had pealed out in the immediate wake of the Finney revivals.

BURNOUT

One reason for this lack of focus in Christian abolitionism was the changing convictions of early abolitionist leaders. A considerable body of revivalistic evangelicals did sustain the antislavery testimony in the decades before the Civil War. Oberlin, with Charles Finney always an important influence, sent forth numerous workers against slavery, some helping fugitive slaves escape to Canada, others continuing to promote abolitionism through lectures, tracts, and newspapers. Finney himself committed more and more time to expounding his theology and, eventually, to evangelistic trips to Great Britain. But he never lost the sharp edge of his antislavery feeling. In 1846 he could say, "No generation before us ever had the light on the evils and wrongs of Slavery that we have: hence our guilt exceeds that of any former generation of slave holders; and, moreover, knowing all the cruel wrongs and miseries of the system from the history of the past, every persisting slave-holder endorses all the crimes and assumes all the guilt involved in the system and evolved out of it since the world began."[22] Finney never could support Abraham Lincoln, because he felt Lincoln's stand against slavery was too cautious.

For other early leaders of revivalistic abolition, however, the strain to keep together evangelical piety and fervor for social reform became too great. A historian of "the Lane rebellion," in which Theodore Dwight Weld led antislavery students from the seminary in Cincinnati to Oberlin College, traced the later career of the Lane rebels and came to this conclusion: "The conflict in the relationship between evangelicalism and antislavery had several ramifications. Some of the rebels gave up the antislavery of the Lane debate and rebellion for evangelicalism. Others discarded much of evangelicalism in favor of antislavery and reform. Weld, and perhaps others, gave up both."[23] The later careers of Weld and of William Lloyd Garrison are of greatest interest in showing these sort of changes.

For Weld, both antislavery and evangelical Protestantism proved too strenuous to bear. After his activity in Washington in the early 1840s as a lobbyist for abolition, he in effect retired from public view. For much of the rest of his life, he conducted a private school where the emphasis was upon inner spirituality and self-control rather than on public action. In addition, his friends from the days of the Finney revivals grew increasingly concerned as they saw him discard first one, and then another, of traditional Protestant beliefs. Weld did not teach the Scriptures to his students; he dabbled with several forms of spiritualism over the last decades of his life; and he was buried in a Unitarian church. Disenchantment with the religion of Charles Finney accompanied disenchantment with the Christian activism that religion promoted. Robert Abzug, a recent biographer, summarizes succinctly the turn from earlier ways that characterized Weld from the 1840s on:

As for his life in reform, a life he had pursued for twenty years, he left it in exhaustion and disillusionment. His leaving can be explained only partially by external events. It is true that the antislavery cause had experienced major setbacks, and belief in a quick end to the institution through moral suasion had long since vanished. Yet others fought on and new converts entered the field every year. Besides, in the past Theodore had faced setbacks squarely and had gone on to fight harder. This time, however, he was listening to an inner voice that conceded that the cosmic vision that had made him a reformer was in error. . . . The evangelical vision had dominated Weld's life since his conversion under Finney twenty years prior. In that tumultuous episode, his senses of identity and calling became fused with the Finneyite mission— reform and conversion of the world to bring on the millennial age—and that fusion unleased an almost mythic power in this energetic man. Failure and division in the antislavery movement, . . . , and a halting recognition of deep emotional starvation—all had allowed Weld the chance slowly to separate his self from evangelical mission. His trips to Washington provided a final test for the old calling, and in the end he did not hear the call.[24]

For Weld, and at least a few other early reformers, the goal had been too high and the effort had cost too much.

Quite different was William Lloyd Garrison, who remained to the end an ardent foe of slavery. In his case, it was not reform as such that gave way, but the link with evangelical Protestantism. Garrison came more and more to feel that Southern Bible expositors might be correct. Scripture, especially the Old Testament, did seem to allow for slavery. If that was the case, then there must be a problem with the traditional Protestant confidence in the Bible. By 1849 he could write in *The Liberator,* "To say that everything contained within the lids of the bible is divinely inspired, and to insist upon the dogma as fundamentally important, is to give utterance to a bold fiction, and to require the suspension of the reasoning faculties. To say that everything in the bible is to be believed, simply because it is found in that volume, is equally absurd and pernicious."[25] For Garrison, the choice was clear. When abolitionism and the Scriptures conflict, abandon the Scriptures.

As abolition suffered throughout the 1840s at the hands of the politicians, Garrison reacted almost as strongly against the national ideals that sustained many of his fellow workers. As he came to view it, the Constitution was a blot on the national conscience. Because of its several provisions protecting slavery, it amounted to "a covenant with death and an agreement with Hell." Later he would actually burn the document and say over the flames, "So perish all compromises with tyranny."[26] Garrison never relinquished his revivalistic fervor, but he did eventually exclude from its purview the evangelical Protestantism and the veneration for the nation's founding documents that continued to be so much a part of Christian political action in his day and since.

A sharp contrast to Garrison and Weld is offered by the activities of black abolitionists in the North, many of whom were also inspired by Christian convictions. Their position was never as secure as that of whites and after 1850 became even more precarious when a new Fugitive Slave Law allowed Southerners to seek out escaped slaves in the

North. Yet despite great obstacles, including systematic social prejudice in the North, many black abolitionists persevered. The ex-slave Frederick Douglass was the best known, but many others continued the fight even when white supporters turned aside and political conditions seemed to worsen.[27]

Weld and Garrison were not necessarily representative of all white abolitionists. But their careers do suggest the strains of revivalist abolitionism. Without the immediate success to which the rhetoric of revival pointed, it was not altogether surprising that, at least for some reformers, the synthesis of revival and reform did not hold.

THE CIVIL WAR AND THE END OF SLAVERY

Revivalistic abolitionism raised the issue of slavery to national attention, but it was the force of arms and political compromise that brought about an end to the slave system. Long-time abolitionists added their voice to the Northern crusade for the Union that eventually defeated the Confederacy and terminated slavery. With the passage of the Thirteenth Amendment and its prohibition of slavery in December 1865, leading abolitionists felt their job was over. Garrison stopped publishing *The Liberator*. With the passage of the Fifteenth Amendment in 1870, guaranteeing ex-slaves the right to vote, the American Anti-Slavery Society disbanded. Most abolitionists traded in their earlier moral fervor for a more pragmatic approach to the times and its needs.

Slavery was at an end, but of course the racism and systemic oppression of black people continued. Jim Crow laws in the South, lynch mobs North and South, would replace the formal institutions of slavery to render most of the nation's blacks second-class citizens at best. The Civil War, like so many other wars in the history of nations, proved to be a powerful solvent of moral reform. The issue of slavery formally solved, Christians turned to other concerns. Some looked eagerly to the fruits of a new wave of evangelism, this time under the inspiration of Dwight L. Moody. Others struggled to make the gospel speak to the changing social conditions of an industrial America. A few were inching toward the contrasting conceptions of the Christian faith that would lead to the Fundamentalist-Modernist controversy. Political concern for the liberty of America's black citizens would not arise among the white churches for nearly a century.

In short, the crusade against slavery had won, and it had lost. The proper laws were now in place, but the reality of freedom for America's blacks still struggled to be born. After the Civil War, that struggle was not of major interest to the nation's white Christians. By 1865 the antislavery revival was over.

8. The Promise and Peril of Reform II: Prohibition

The movement to restrict, and later to ban, the sale and possession of alcholic beverages bears many similarities to the drive against slavery. In both cases Christian arguments were joined with more generally humanitarian reasoning to make the case for a wide-ranging social reform. In both, the Second Great Awakening was the occasion for mobilizing personal convictions against a social evil. In both, the effort to achieve reform through personal rehabilitation imperceptibly crossed the line into political action. In both, the mobilization of reform brought about significant social betterment. Finally, in both, the good that was accomplished was balanced by unexpected results in society and for the Christian faith.

WINE TO GLADDEN THE HEART

The historical Christian position on alcoholic beverages had always been temperance, defined by the normal use of the term. Within Orthodox, Catholic, and Protestant churches until the eighteenth century, moderate use of fermented beverages was rarely considered a problem in itself. The Church's stand against drunkenness was consistent, but so was its untroubled attitude toward moderate imbibing. Later in American history, prohibitionists like the evangelist Billy Sunday would latch onto Bible passages like Proverbs 20:1 ("Wine is a mocker, strong drink a brawler; and whoever is led astray by it is not wise") to advance their efforts. Much more prominent in earlier Christian thinking were the words of the psalmist who could praise God for providing fermentation: "Thou dost cause the grass to grow for the cattle, and plants for man to cultivate, that he may bring forth food from the earth, and wine to gladden the heart of man." (Ps. 104:14–15)

To sum up, most Christians before 1800 regarded the moderate use of alcoholic beverages—especially wine, cider, beer, and other drinks produced by natural fermentation—as a gracious gift from God. After 1800 more and more Americans came to look on the use of alcoholic drinks—especially liquors produced by the process of distillation—as a dreadful evil deserving the most strenuous opposition.

In the early days of American settlement, Christians, no less than other colonists, provided themselves with fermented spirits. The persecuted Pilgrims carried an ample supply of "hot water," as they called it, when they arrived aboard the *Mayflower* in 1620. The pious Reverend Francis Higginson embarked for Massachusetts Bay in 1629 with forty-five casks of beer and twenty gallons of brandy for the use of his family and the wider Puritan community.[1] By 1670 the cultivation of apples had advanced to the point where from New England to Virginia hard cider, or applejack, became standard fare at public gatherings, including many church affairs. Other drinks were also taken for granted. When Jonathan Edwards's father was ordained a pastor in 1698, for example, provisions for the festivities included fourteen pounds of mutton, eighty-eight pounds of beef, four quarts of rum, and eight quarts of wine.

The Puritans of New England did take corrective action against the overindulgent. The stocks, or even a public whipping, awaited those whose excessive drinking led to public disturbances or domestic violence. In the early 1700s the venerable Cotton Mather spoke from the pulpit against the immoderate use of alchohol, particularly the excessive tippling that went on when local militia companies gathered for Training Days. He was also concerned that drunkenness was rendering the Indians incapable of receiving the gospel message. Yet Mather too looked upon the milder forms of liquor as good gifts of the Creator to the creature. Some historians think it was Mather who coined the old New England proverb, "Wine is from God, but drunkenness from the devil." If so, he was echoing the words of his father, Increase Mather, another dignified Boston clergymen, from 1673, "Drink is in itself a creature of God, and to be received with thankfulness."[2] In short, almost no one in colonial America felt any tension between Christianity and the moderate use of alcohol. Of the Scotch-Irish who came to American from Londonderry, Ireland, for example, it was said: "The Derry Presbyterians never give up a pint [i.e., point] of doctrine, nor a pint of rum."

The ready use of liquor by colonial Americans had much to do with their living conditions. The colonial diet was monotonous; settlers ate great quantities of meat that had been preserved by salting; lives were filled with hardship and disease; wine and cider were widely thought to be of general medicinal value; and there was no central heating. In addition, by the mid-eighteenth century the trade in the raw materials of rum manufacturing (sugar and molasses) and in rum itself had come to be an important part of colonial economic life. Venerated patriots like Sam Adams, John Hancock, and Paul Revere were only some of the leaders who engaged in the sometimes illegal, but highly profitable, rum traffic with the West Indies and Africa. Well into the nineteenth century, America's cities often lacked plentiful and healthful sources of drinking water. Moderate consumption of alcoholic beverages was not only accepted, but often was also the only practical solution to the lack of good water.

AMERICA'S DRINKING PROBLEM AND THE REVIVAL

Reaction to the use of alcohol set in with the altered circumstances of the early nineteenth century.[3] It was not just the wild imaginations of temperance reformers that perceived Americans drinking more, and more destructively. Steady advance in the technology of distillation, an increasing tendency toward social acceptance of heavy indulgence, and the growing willingness of farmers to convert their grain into alcoholic beverages as a way of bringing produce to market all contributed to a major increase in the consumption of alcohol after the Revolutionary War. The historian W. J. Rorabaugh has estimated that the consumption of alcohol (figured in absolute terms by calculating percentages of alcohol in the distilled liquors and fermented beverages actually consumed) rose from five to six gallons per capita in the period 1710–1790 to over seven gallons per capita in the years 1795 to 1830.[4] Moreover, the increase in consumption was especially noticeable at public occasions or group gatherings, where drinking to excess seemed to be becoming the norm. In the early nineteenth century, in other words, America had a drinking problem. It was a problem threatening social decay and special destruction for the family. "Alcohol was pervasive in American society," wrote Rorabaugh,

it crossed regional, sexual, racial, and class lines. Americans drank at home and abroad, alone and together, at work and at play, in fun and in earnest. They drank from the crack of dawn to the crack of dawn. At nights taverns were filled with boisterous, mirth-making tipplers. Americans drank before meals, with meals, and after meals. They drank while working in the fields and while travelling across half a continent. They drank in their youth, and, if they lived long enough, in their old age. They drank at formal events, such as weddings, ministerial ordinations, and wakes, and on no occasion—by the fireside of an evening, on a hot afternoon, when the mood called. From sophisticated Andover to frontier Illinois, from Ohio to Georgia, in lumbercamps and on satin settees, in log taverns and at fashionable New York hotels, the American greeting was, "Come, Sir, take a dram first." Seldom was it refused.[5]

Before long, the increase in drinking was matched by an increase in Christian sensitivity to the issue. Here the revival of religion in the Second Great Awakening played a large role. An early sign of temperance concern was revival leaders' distaste for the practice. One of the most prominent New England revivalists, Lyman Beecher, once wrote disgustedly of a meeting of Connecticut ministers that was marred by the unseemly use of alcohol: "The sideboard with the spillings of water, and sugar, and liquor, looked and smelled like the bar of a very active grogshop." In Beecher's opinion, such use of alcohol befogged the minds and contaminated the spirits of the Connecticut ministers; it was "nullifying the means of grace."[6]

Though Beecher had his differences with Charles Finney over details of revival practice, he joined Finney and other revivalists in laboring diligently for both the conversion and the reform of the American population. Like Finney, Beecher's concern for the American character went along with his concern for the spread of the gospel. To Beecher, Finney, and like-minded revivalists, overindulgence in drink was looming ever larger as a threat to Christianity and to Christian civilization. Drinking was harmful to what they saw as traditional Anglo-

Saxon virtues, but it also seemed to be a sign of the growing presence of Catholic and non-Christian immigrants in America. To the revivalists, the campaign for temperance grew even more naturally out of the basic message of Christianity than did the drive against slavery. And so it came about, as the historian Ronald Walters summarizes the situation, "In the antebellum years at least, [temperance reform] attracted the largest, most diverse collection of supporters of any reform."[7]

Beecher himself set out the case against "ardent spirits" in a hard-hitting book first published in 1826. Its title summed up its contents very well: *Six Sermons on the Nature, Occasion, Signs, Evils, and Remedy of Intemperance.* Beverage alcohol, for Beecher, stood condemned because of the harm it did to "the health and physical energies of a nation," to the "national intellect," to the "military prowess of a nation," to the "patriotism of a nation," to the "national conscience or moral principle," to the "national industry," and to "civil liberty." Beecher's greatest concern, however, was "the moral ruin [liquor] works in the soul." For Beecher and the growing number of Protestant reformers who stood with him, liquor reform was a major part of the effort to smooth the way for the gospel and to improve American society.

TEMPERANCE OR PROHIBITION?

Several specific issues confronted temperance advocates in their crusade. The first concerned the very name under which they operated. Were they in fact "temperance" reformers or "prohibitionists"? Should their reform be directed toward moderation in the use of alcoholic beverages or to total abstinence? As early as 1780 American Methodists declared themselves for total abstinence, but that was a minority position at the time. The first voluntary temperance society in Connecticut, established at Litchfield in 1789, argued only for moderation. By 1830, however, the balance had tipped. Following such advice as Beecher's in *Six Sermons,* for example, the American Temperance Society in 1826 went on record for total abstinence. As Beecher put it, "There is no prudent use of ardent spirits, but when it is used as a medicine."[8]

This point of view, to make a bad pun, did not go down easily, particularly on the frontier. In tiny New Salem, Illinois, for example, some of the citizens were confirmed teetotalers, including young Abraham Lincoln, who had had several disquieting experiences with drink. But Dr. John Allen, founder of the New Salem temperance society as well as of its debating society and Sunday school, "found his worst opponents among the church members, most of whom had their barrels of whiskey at home."[9]

WHAT IS AN "INTOXICATING LIQUOR"?

A second issue had to do not so much with temperance or abstinence, as with what counted as beverage alcohol. Many believers who would have condemned the New Salem whiskey drinkers had their doubts about less intoxicating drinks. Benjamin Rush, the Philadelphia physician who led many reform efforts in the Revolutionary period, published in 1784 *An Inquiry into the Effects of Spiritous Liquors on the Human Body and Mind.* This widely reprinted tract condemned the use of distilled liquors in strongest terms. Rush believed, however, that beer, wine, and cider in moderation exerted a positive effect on personal health and social well-being. When Lyman Beecher first spoke out against intemperance, he made no mention of wine or beer, because he knew that many Christians considered them acceptable beverages. Yet gradually these milder forms of fermented alcohol fell under condemnation also. So effective was the drive to suppress all forms of drink that even the White House went "dry" for a few years after the Civil War. "Lemonade Lucy" Hays (a Methodist) and Mrs. James Garfield (of the Disciples of Christ) served no alcohol of any kind at presidential functions. Thus, from 1876 to 1881 the temperance crusade conquered the White House, where, in the words of a visiting statesmen, "the water flowed like champagne."

Later this same uncertainty as to what constitutes beverage alcohol lent some ambiguity to the Eighteenth Amendment of 1919. It prohibited explicitly "intoxicating liquors," but left it to Congress to define which beverages fell into that category. In the Volsted Act of 1919, Congress stipulated that .5% alcohol content constituted an "intoxicating liquor." Some students of the prohibition era think that a narrower concentration on distilled liquor might have done a great deal to preserve the popular support that led to national prohibition in 1919 but quickly dissipated in the 1920s.

THE COMMUNION QUESTION

A third related issue was "the communion question." Would the practices of centuries of Christianity be altered to exclude fermented wine from the celebration of the Lord's Supper? Nowhere was the ultraism of the prohibition movement more evident than on this question, for as sentiment against drink grew, so also did the effort to demonstrate the Bible's full support for teetotalism. A considerable number of Bible commentators even attempted to interpret the "wine" of Scripture as an unfermented drink. It was not long before grape juice replaced wine in many Baptist, Presbyterian, Disciples, Mennonite, and other churches—especially when technological advances after the Civil War made it possible to preserve (and of course to market) the juice of grapes in unfermented form.

A few Christians held out, with the argument that the Bible knew nothing of such extreme views. The Reverend Thomas Laurie defended the traditional practice with these words from 1869: "Has it not been shown from the established meaning of the word, from the customs of Bible lands, and from the testimony of holy scripture, that wine is the fermented juice of the grape, and that such is the element appointed by the Saviour to be the memorial of his blood in the sacrament of the supper."[10] But spokesmen like Laurie found it more and more difficult to gain a hearing for their views among fervent Protestants.

THE BIBLE

Much the more common position in the mid-nineteenth century was the position argued by leaders among Baptists, Methodists, Presbyterians, and other denominations. The Bible, it seemed, had been misinterpreted for centuries. Scripture taught total abstinence from drink, even from the use of feremented wine at communion. The effort to prove such points took the form of learned disquisitions on the words commonly translated "wine" in the Bible, such as found in the articles "Bible and Drink" (by F. R. Lees) and "Bible Wines" (by G. W.

Samson) in the 1891 *Cyclopedia of Temperance and Prohibition*. As Samson summarized his case, the "wine" praised by Old Testament writers was "the fresh grape-juice now pressed into the 'overrunning cup' in Southern France, Spain, and Italy, and also brought now fresh and unfermented from Mediterranean ports to New York"; as for the New Testament, "the wine Christ drank in life was the pure fruit of the vine."[11]

Such arguments had long been developing in the American temperance movement, as had other interpretations of Scripture supporting the cause. The Reverend William Thayer, for example, responded directly to Thomas Laurie's defense of wine in communion, not only by showing that Laurie had misinterpreted Scripture, but by reducing his opponent's arguments to their absurd conclusions: "If Christ commands us to use alcoholic wine at the communion," wrote Thayer against Laurie, "and we cannot celebrate the Lord's Supper properly without it, then *alcohol* is indispensable to the proper observance of this solemn rite. No matter how much of the Divine Spirit the communicant may possess, unless the table is furnished with that other *spirit* which intoxicates, he cannot celebrate our Lord's dying love acceptably."[12]

Temperance advocates also argued strenuously that Scripture explicitly taught total abstinence. A 1868 pamphlet from George Duffield, pastor of the First Presbyterian Church in Detroit, was typical of many such efforts. As Duffield saw it, "total abstinence from all intoxicating drink is the Bible rule of Temperance." As he expanded on that theme the connections between temperance reform and the spirit of the Second Great Awakening are quite clear:

Total abstinence from that which is evil, unlawful, sinful, is the radical idea of Temperance. It is part and parcel of self-denial, self-control, self-government, by whatever name we choose to call it. The extent to which this abstinence is required, the apostle has decided. All sorts or forms of evil are to be avoided. "Abstain from all appearance of evil." I Thess. v. 22. The moderate use or indulgence of anything, morally or physically evil, can lay no claim to be accounted Temperance, according to the meaning of *enchrateia*. Before it can be justly claimed that the moderate use of wine or of any intoxicating liquor is Temperance, it must be shown that such liquors are legitimate means to be used for gratifying appetite. If God has disapproved of intoxicating drink or wine; if he has condemned it as an odious, horrible evil; and especially, if by any precept or precedent, he has prohibited its use,—then, according to the Bible, total abstinence is the Temperance appropriate and requisite.[13]

To advocates of the temperance movement arising out of American revivalism, it was increasingly clear that the weighty voice of Scripture supported the crusade against drink.

THE TURN TO POLITICS

The last question was strategic. How should a reform in drinking habits be accomplished? The answer to this query bridged the private world of revivalistic conversion and the public world of political behavior. In its first decades, the temperance movement shunned overt political action. The goal, rather, was to convert individuals through the preaching of the gospel, and then to show the dangers of drink to redeemed individuals, who would be expected to see the logic of temperance and then leave drinking behind. This picture of reform prevailed in the American Temperance Society and among the well-educated, articulate clergymen who directed its activities. It was also the view of more popular movements, like the Washington Temperance Societies. From the early 1840s the Washingtonians used festive rallies and populist literature to enlist laboring men, and especially reformed alcoholics, in the cause. Their goal was to see as many people as possible "take the pledge" to become total abstainers.

The personal approach to temperance reform had considerable effect. As the decades passed, Americans did begin to drink less and to be more aware of the dangers of overindulgence. Again to use the statistics of W. J. Rorabaugh, the per capita consumption of absolute alcohol for Americans over age fifteen dropped from 7.1 gallons in 1830 to 3.1 gallons in 1840.[14]

Even as revivalists and reformers promoted individual action against drink, however, the move toward organized political action had begun.

In 1838, temperance reformers convinced the Massachusetts legislature to pass a law prohibiting the sale of distilled liquor in quantities less than fifteen gallons. This act was effective in taking hard liquor out of the taverns and restricting its circulation to the very few individuals with enough money to purchase such quantities. Soon other reformers followed Massachusetts' example.

In Maine, the active cooperation of abolitionists and the dedicated leadership of Neal Dow led to even stronger measures. Maine's abolitionists shared a background in evangelical revivalism with its prohibitionists, and so were easily persuaded to lend their media skills and experience in political persuasion to the fight against alcohol. Neal Dow (1804–1897) was an energetic reformer who had been won to the cause by Lyman Beecher and who used political pressure and, eventually, his office as mayor of Portland, to campaign for prohibition. After a series of lesser successes, the Maine reformers achieved their goal in 1851, when the state legislature passed a measure prohibiting the sale and manufacturing of all alcoholic beverages in the state.

The Maine law became a model for later political activity on both the state and local level. Already in the 1850s, all the other New England states passed similar statutes, as did New York and several midwestern states. A variety of circumstances, including court challenges and shifting political fortunes in the state legislatures, led to the rapid overturning of many of these earlier statewide prohibitions. But the taste of victory had been captivating, and temperance reformers continued their work.

Efforts in New England to promote a moral society through political action had a far-ranging effect on general efforts to reform American society. Under early leaders like Finney and Beecher, temperance reform had been carried out as a parallel to religious revival. Just as in revival the key was to touch the heart of the individual, so in temperance reform the key was persuasion of the individual. Soon, however, temperance reformers experienced the same transformation as the abolitionists had. If individuals would not embrace a reform for their own good, then it was the duty of public-spirited leaders to secure the desired end through political means. The major difference between

the abolition and the temperance movements was that the prohibitionists had much more success. And victories gained through the political
process continued well into the twentieth century.

Victory did not, however, extend to grander political goals. Soon
after the Civil War, a number of temperance advocates proposed a
political party to promote their cause. Accordingly, a convention was
held in Chicago in 1869 to decide on further political action. To suggest
the way in which temperance reform was tied into other reforming
impulses of the period, it is instructive to note that this was the nation's
first political convention in which women participated as equals. The
first candidate of the Prohibitionist party garnered nearly 6,000 votes
in the 1872 race, and a standard-bearer for the party has run in every
presidential election since then. At the height of populist reform at the
end of the nineteenth century, the party's presidential candidates gained
as many as 270,000 votes (in 1892, over 2 percent of the total cast). But
support was dwindling even before passage of the Eighteenth Amendment. After the passage of the prohibition amendment and its repeal,
the vote totals for the Prohibitionist candidate declined dramatically,
so that since 1924 the party has never received as much as one-quarter
of one percent of the national total; since 1956 no candidate has received
as much as one-tenth of one percent.[15]

If the Prohibition party had its difficulties, however, there were
enough triumphs to be had working through previously established
channels. The successes, both actual and anticipated, of the temperance
movement were crucial for Christian political action. They held out
the prospect that political organization—arising from a moral vision
and resulting in a political strategy—could really work. The historian
Ronald Walters does not exaggerate when he speaks of temperance
political activity as "the most important thing for the history of
[American] reform." As Walters explains this judgment: "More than
slavery, [the victories of prohibition] convinced reformers not to rely
exclusively upon moral suasion. The fifteen-gallon and Maine laws
were proof that vices might be legislated away more easily than sinners
could be converted."[16] That, at least, was the grail that beckoned
invitingly to Christian social activists throughout the nineteenth century and into the twentieth.

TOWARD NATIONAL PROHIBITION

For most of the century before 1919, the Methodist church, with its strong perfectionist bent, spearheaded the drive to outlaw all forms of alcoholic beverage. The Women's Christian Temperance Union under the dynamic leadership of Frances Willard, the Anti-Saloon League, and other societies that combined moral suasion and political lobbying gave broad public impetus to the drive. These largely Protestant organizations also received considerable assistance from some members of the Roman Catholic hierarchy, who in addition wanted to prove themselves good Americans and disabuse their fellow citizens of the notion that Catholics were anti-American and loose-living. The drive for prohibition also was very successful in crossing theological lines. Conservative believers, who insisted upon the traditional character of the Christian faith, were joined by proponents of the Social Gospel, who often were more willing to adjust the faith to more recent intellectual conventions. Both, however, could agree to pursue politically the vision of a drink-free, responsible American society.

The events of World War I heightened American fears of social disorder and paved the way for the prohibition amendment to the Constitution. Growing fears about the evil effects of drink on the unsavory elements in American society combined with a propensity to link the crimes of the Kaiser's Germany with the evils of drink. These twentieth-century developments added fuel to the prohibitionist flame that had been ignited in the previous century. The Eighteenth Amendment to the Constitution of 1919 was the result. The war had shown how fragile civilization itself was and seemed to spotlight the need for more strenuous measures toward social discipline. In this belief Americans were joined by citizens from Canada, Great Britain, and several other European nations, all of which passed temperance or prohibitionist legislation around the same time.[17] With the prohibition amendment, the promise of the Maine law seemed to be fulfilled. Political action for moral purposes had won the day.

When the Eighteenth Amendment and its prohibition of "the manufacture, sale, or transportation of intoxicating liquors" took effect on

January 17, 1920, some Christians heralded the bright dawning of a new era. In Norfolk, Virginia, the revivalist Billy Sunday staged a funeral service for "John Barleycorn." His speech summed up the aspirations that had led to so much Christian political action against the trade in alcohol. "Good-by, John," the revivalist said, "the reign of tears is over. . . . The slums will soon be only a memory. We will turn our prisons into factories and our jails into storehouses and corncribs. Men will walk upright now, women will smile, and the children will laugh. Hell will be forever rent."[18]

THE FAILURE OF NATIONAL PROHIBITION

As it turned out, the brief era of national prohibition had some positive benefit for the health of the country. The rate of drinking, as well as crimes related to drunkenness, declined. Alcoholism was less obviously a problem in many communities. And energies directed toward the achievement of the Eighteenth Amendment were free to be employed elsewhere.

At the same time, national prohibition failed as a political policy. The government itself was unwilling to provide adequate support for the ban, perhaps out of simple lack of will, perhaps because of a traditional American wariness about meddling in the private lives of citizens. Influential journalists and other decision makers highlighted the growth in crime related to rum-running, speakeasies, and gang warfare over the control of the illegal liquor traffic. Young people, especially in urban areas, seemed to find illegal drinking a fascinating temptation for proving their maturity. Immigrant communities, where the consumption of alcoholic beverages was an accepted part of family culture, added their voice to the call for repeal. After only a few years, all but the most ardent defenders of prohibition realized that it did not amount to the social fix-all that its earlier proponents had advertised.

The result was the Twenty-first Amendment in 1933, which ended the "noble experiment." In America drinking became again a matter of personal judgment, Christians retreated to moral arguments or directed political energies to state and local venues, and government increasingly assumed the major responsibility for dealing with the major social problems of alcoholism and drunkenness. The "temperance" crusade, in which Christians had played such an important role, had come to the end.

Christian efforts to abolish slavery and to encourage temperance were noble efforts. They deserve careful consideration in order to spell out exactly what they contributed to American life and how they related to the course of Christianity on these shores. They deserve just as careful scrutiny for the weaknesses they reveal in the characteristic patterns of American Christian political action. The next chapter, which considers also the lessons to be learned from the other episodes we have examined, attempts such an analysis. That analysis, in turn, will put us in a position to examine, much more briefly, several significant moments of Christian political activity in the twentieth century.

III. PRINCIPLES

9. The Lessons of History

The reform movements directed against slavery and drink highlight several important features of Christian political action in America. Roughly the same generalizations that hold true for reform movements apply to other episodes of our history in which Christians have participated directly in the political sphere. The task in this chapter is to spell out those generalizations, to weigh up pluses and minuses, and to assess reasons for the successes and failures of Christian political action. This exercise in turn will point us toward questions of principle—religious and political—that can be of use for orienting Christian political activity in the present.

AMERICAN CHRISTIAN POLITICS

Christian politics has existed on four levels in American history. Principles, values, convictions, and beliefs derived from Christian faith have, at the first level, provided the framework for political reflection and action.

On a second level, Christians have mobilized publicly to promote specific projects or the reform of specific abuses. As such, their activity has been political in a general sense, not necessarily directed toward legislation or the election of candidates, but toward shaping opinion or changing private behavior. Christian political action of this sort is distinguished by its moral and personal character. Something wrong must be corrected, or something neglected attended to, but an improvement is expected from specific changes in the lives and moral values of countless individuals.

On a third level, Christian action moves from personal to more explicitly political persuasion. Here the goal is the translation of a moral agenda, rooted in Christian convictions, into positive legislation (or even a change in the Constitution). At this level, Christian action begins to look like interest group politics more generally. Petitions, lobbying, informal caucuses inside and outside government, legal battles before the courts, formal organizations with paid staff, and other of the myriad ways by which American constituents influence their elected leaders come into play at this stage.

A fourth and final level of activity is the creation of political parties designed expressly to transform a general Christian impulse into political organization of the sort that has characterized the Democrats and the Republicans. At this stage, the aspiration is to gain political power, or at least to secure recognition for a Christian point of view, through mobilization at the broadest and most comprehensive level.

As a general rule, Christian politics has been most beneficial—in terms both of actual political influence and of fidelity to the Christian faith—at the level of general conviction. It has done most poorly—again in terms of both politics and Christianity—in the effort to create complete political parties around an individual or a set of Christian convictions. The record for activity at the intervening levels—personal moral persuasion and political mobilization for specific legislative purposes—is mixed, with some examples both of commendable and of problematic Christian activity.

POLITICAL PARTIES

For better or for worse, Christian political parties have simply not worked in America. The Liberty party in 1840 and 1844, the Prohibition party (which has fielded a national nominee every four years since 1872), the Anti-Masonic party of 1832 (which arose in fearful alarm at the spread of Masonry in the North), and the American or "Know-Nothing" party of 1856 (whose principal platform was the restriction of Catholic immigration into America) were all organized in order to promote a specific political agenda thought to arise out of the Christian faith itself. As political organizations, these Christian parties have been either short-lived and unstable (Liberty, Anti-Masonic, American) or if long-lived, quite ineffective (Prohibition).

More important than a lack of political effect, however, is the problem of Christian witness. The leaders of these parties have tended toward paranoia in their outlook on the world; they have defined "the

Christian position" with extreme narrowness; they have largely for-saken responsibility for the general course of political affairs; and they have often used unchristian tactics (especially that of playing on the fears of their followers with regard to fanciful conspiracies) as a way of promoting their goals. In the modern history of Europe, political parties organized around Christian principles—in some cases Protes-tant, in others Roman Catholic—offer good examples of seeking power and expressing Christian principles, but in America, similar ventures have merely led Christians down a blind alley.

POLITICAL REFORM

The American record of Christian organization for specific political goals, pursued self-consciously as an expression of Christian conviction, is considerably better. This judgment may be offered both for prepoliti-cal individual moral persuasion and for more self-consciously political action. In fact, as we have seen in the sketches of both abolition and prohibition, it is difficult to distinguish between the more general and more specific types of political action, since in our American setting personal moral persuasion so often and so easily moves over into explicitly political activity. The examples of this activity—whether general and persuasive or organized and electoral—have been in many ways both effective as politics and faithful as Christian witness. From such well-intentioned action comes much of the justification for re-garding America as a "Christian country" in the qualified, restricted sense of the term.

This is not to say that efforts by American Christians to shape public life according to their convictions have been free from difficulty. To the contrary, there have been many problems in such efforts. And they have been serious problems, as the following list suggests:

(1) American Christians have often been quixotic, at best, when selecting causes for political action. The way in which, for example, Protestants in the 1850s could come to see political opposition to Catholic immigration as a *religious* issue, or that retention of the Panama Canal in the 1970s became a cause for specifically *Christian* concern, illustrates this problem.

(2) American Christians have often overestimated the benefits to be

gained from securing a particular political goal. The crusades for abolition and prohibition both show that it was much easier to pass legislation, and even to amend the Constitution, than to change the deeply engrained habits against which believers protested.

(3) American Christians have occasionally committed themselves so intensely to the achievement of a religiously defined political goal that failure to reach that goal brings disillusion or despair. Millennial visions have raised Christian activism to great heights but have also set up the activists for a tremendous fall.

(4) American Christians have too often pursued Christian political ends with unchristian political means. Debate over the Bible's implications for slavery in the 1840s and over the scriptural teaching on the use of fermented beverages in the 1920s are only two occasions when Christian antagonists used every means, foul as well as fair, to advance their political goals.

(5) American Christians have sometimes applied Christian political reasoning with wooden insensitivity to the election of their political leaders. The presidential campaign of 1800 is not the only instance when the political deployment of Christian principles (perhaps justifiable narrowly on their own terms) harmed rather than helped the general state of society.

(6) Finally, American Christians have often sold their faith captive to the intense political needs of the moment. The War for Independence and the Civil War, when combatants on both sides identified their cause unhesitatingly with the Christian faith itself, are probably the most obvious examples of such blundering. But the same thing has occurred much more frequently whenever other compelling political issues were equated with the essence of the faith.

Notwithstanding these significant difficulties, however, American Christians still have a remarkable record of faithful political behavior. This kind of action has laid the foundation for public values now widely taken for granted in American life. Such values include the expectation that public officials will exercise their offices morally, an expectation nurtured by specific Christian insistence in our Revolutionary era. It includes the belief that government may not disregard the essential humanity of its citizens, a proposition reiterated by Christians in any number of circumstances throughout our history.

Of such examples, however, the most important is the respect enshrined in American law for individuals of all races and colors. Without pretending to minimize Christian defenses of slavery or support given by Christians to other oppressive laws and social conditions, it still is the case that for the first century after the American Revolution, Christians provided the central, and sometimes the only, moral opposition to the system of chattel bondage. It is also the case that Christians, especially the descendants of the slaves, played an immensely significant role in twentieth-century efforts to broaden political rights for blacks and then for all citizens. Again, although there are important exceptions, the Christian record of political mobilization in behalf of marginalized or disenfranchised members of society—from women, children, factory workers, the physically handicapped, and the mentally ill in the nineteenth century, to the unborn, the aged, and the terminally ill in our present generation—is praiseworthy in the strongest terms. Take away these Christian influences in our political history, and we lose much of what makes America attractively distinctive in the history of modern nations.

Christian political action has also been laudable in venues that have not been so widely honored or acknowledged. For example, the temperance movement, for all its foibles, deserves much more than the humerous scorn with which it is often described. Christian opposition to intemperance, especially in light of current knowledge, should be a mark of good sense and wise social policy rather than a cause for embarrassment. More clearly than even the ardent teetotalers of the nineteenth century, we now realize the social cost of alcoholism, the carnage wreaked by drunken drivers, and the peril to our young people from overindulgence. Christians may have been guilty of sensationalizing the dangers of drink and of seeking inappropriate political solutions to the abuse of alcohol, but both the general case for moderation and the Christian promotion of that cause deserve much better than they have received in the historical record.

In addition, American political activity by Christians in defense of human rights or in pursuit of social change includes noteworthy, if largely forgotten episodes. The failure of such activity, or its evolution into programs dominated by secular intent, sometimes obscures its significance. Three examples, featuring believers with different conceptions of the Christian faith, can make the point.

In the 1830s, evangelical Protestant missionaries in Georgia protested, and then attempted coordinated political activity, when the national government began to force the Cherokees out of the lands to which they were legally entitled.[1] The protests were made with conviction and integrity, but they were unavailing. The Cherokees were banished across the Mississippi; the significant civilization established by the Indians was ruined; and the protesting missionaries were utterly defeated.

A decade later, Catholic bishops in Philadelphia and New York asked city officials responsible for public education to respect the religious rights of Catholic children in the schools.[2] The bishops wanted the Catholic students to be able to read the Bible in translations approved by their church. Again, their honorable political protests, carried out with dignity through proper channels, were rebuffed, and public education remained for another generation or more under strictly Protestant control.

Toward the end of the nineteenth century in several northern cities, Protestant volunteers (whose theology ranged from moderately conservative to fairly liberal) sought fresh ways to provide badly needed social services for the burgeoning mass of workers.[3] Efforts to provide what we would today call a safety net of social services, like Jane Addams's Hull House in Chicago, grew out of explicitly Christian motives and led to a considerable range of programs to help those who needed it most. The Christian character of such work, however, was obscured by the fact that the efforts were only partially successful, and also by the fact that governmental structures with a more secular orientation eventually assumed the greatest burden for the work undertaken by these early urban reformers. The point in mentioning these three historical instances is to suggest that honorable political action by Christians can be found in many unexpected corners of America's history, if only we know where to look.

POLITICAL PERSPECTIVE

As noteworthy as specific political actions by Christians have been, the most significant Christian contribution to American politics certainly lies at the level of perspective. By its nature, such a judgment must be tentative, for the distance between the core of personal character and the outworking of political action is considerable. Nonetheless, the most pervasive political influence from Christian sources has almost certainly been that arising from the religious values of political activists and the assumptions of the political process itself. In specific cases, Abraham Lincoln and perhaps James Madison, for example, it is obvious that profound reflection on the human condition under God exerted a large and salutary effect on the American political tradition. Something of the same could probably be said about many other political leaders (the famous and the forgotten), who though not, as it were, professionally pious, still showed the effects of a serious religious influence.

It must also be admitted that Christian elements certainly have contributed to harmful or immoral political behavior. This is true for political life in the mainstream, where Christian values have appeared in the most curious conjunction with a bewildering array of morally neutral or positively anti-Christian sentiments. It is also true that Christian elements have been part of the worldviews promoted by many in the long parade of religious anarchists, religious fascists, and religious collectivists who have populated the nether regions of American political history. For good and for ill, in other words, the deepest impact of Christianity on American politics is the most difficult to get at. It resides in regions more accessible to the political philosopher or the sociologist than to the historian.

One thing, however, can be said about this more pervasive, if obscure, influence that is also true for the more obvious record of overt political activity. On both levels the employment of Christian elements in the political process has worked political benefit along with political harm. Likewise, "Christian" political activity has been on some occasions a faithful extension of personal values into the public sphere; on others, it has amounted to a contradiction of the faith.

THE TWENTIETH CENTURY

The historical material we have examined so far has mostly concerned our early national history. But even a brief glance is enough to suggest that earlier patterns have continued to prevail. Events in recent political history, because they remain so close to historical interpreters, are sometimes difficult to evaluate. At the same time, a few examples should be enough to show that Christian political activity in this century has displayed the same characteristics.

WOODROW WILSON

In the first years of the twentieth century the United States enjoyed the service of several political leaders who set their course unabashedly by Christian lights. Of these the most visible were Woodrow Wilson (1856–1924) and William Jennings Bryan (1860–1925). Wilson, the professional academic who went from the presidency of Princeton University to the governorship of New Jersey to the White House in the three brief years from 1910 to 1913, was a reforming Democrat who won the nation's highest office in large part because of his record at cleaning up corruption in New Jersey.[4] As president from 1913 to 1921, however, Wilson made his mark most indelibly in foreign policy. As president, he tried to preserve American neutrality in the early days of the First World War. When the United States then entered the conflict, he defined our effort in noble terms as "making the world safe for democracy." After the war, in the crowning moment of his career, he attempted to establish a new standard for international justice through the Fourteen Points submitted to the peace conference at Versailles, and especially through his plan for a League of Nations.

The important thing here about Wilson's efforts is that they stemmed at least in large measure from a lifelong Christian commitment. He was raised in the home of a southern Presbyterian minister; he had a conversion experience in 1873; he read the Bible and prayed faithfully throughout his life; and he believed (as had Lincoln before him) that the American experience witnessed the fullest manifestation of public Christian values in all of history. As a statesmen, Wilson attempted to flesh out programs of national security and international peace that drew their inspiration from general Christian conceptions of justice and fair play.

Though Wilson's capacities were far above ordinary, the way he set about his political program did in fact repeat the ordinary American pattern. His ideals for both national and international affairs were based on the assumption that general principles of Christian morality could be translated fairly easily into national policy, and that they also could serve as the direct model for international agreement. With this "Reformed" attitude toward political life, Wilson experienced a considerable measure of success in domestic affairs. He was, however, much less successful in international dealings, where his ideals fell afoul of the intransigent realities of Europe's conflicting interests. When Wilson traveled to the peace convention in 1919, great crowds in England and France hailed him as the savior of Western democracy, but the leaders of the other European states spoke of him in private as a naive amateur who could not cope with the realities of historical antagonisms and the practicalities of postwar needs.

Wilson also embodied the revivalistic approach to political action. Once again, vigorous speech making and moral arm-twisting worked fairly well in the early years of his presidency as he addressed domestic problems. But this style failed when he turned to the more complicated task of gaining American acceptance of the League of Nations. Rather than undertaking careful negotiation (and compromise) with the Republicans who controlled the Senate, Wilson took to the stump to campaign for ratification of the Treaty of Versailles and the League. He felt he could win acceptance for his program and its high moral vision by speaking directly to the people. And so Wilson wore himself out crisscrossing the country, making reasoned but also impassioned addresses in halls and from railroad platforms in behalf of the treaty. America's participation in the League became the equivalent of Theodore Dwight Weld's abolition or Neal Dow's prohibition. It was a cause too noble for normal political negotiation, too lofty for compromise. In the end, when the Senate rejected the treaty, Wilson was left a broken and embittered man.

WILLIAM JENNINGS BRYAN

Something of the same fate befell the political aspirations of Wilson's contemporary, William Jennings Bryan (1860–1925).[5] Bryan was a Democratic populist from Nebraska who three times was his party's standard-bearer in presidential campaigns (1896, 1900, 1908) and who then served as secretary of state during Wilson's first term. Like Wilson, Bryan was a dedicated Christian who had been converted as a young man and who saw politics as a forum for promoting principles of general Christian morality. Bryan took a special interest in the welfare of the American farmers and workers who were suffering from the grasp of manipulating financeers and industrialists. His great speech against the tight gold standard at the Democratic convention in 1896 ("You shall not press down upon the brow of labor this crown of thorns, you shall not crucify mankind upon a cross of gold")[6] both summed up his economic policies and revealed the Christian overtones of his thought. Bryan's reformist campaigns on behalf of ordinary American citizens never succeeded, but he was a valiant political warrior who left his mark on a whole generation of American politics.

The reasons for Bryan's failure lay partly in the political climate of the time (Republican policies really did work fairly and beneficially for many urbanites and the citizens of small northern towns) and partly from his own style. Bryan was a crusader, who earned his living between presidential campaigns as an itinerant speaker, and a motivator, whose most famous address was an oft-repeated oration on the example of "The Prince of Peace."

Bryan's goals were undoubtedly worthy ones. With only a few other leading politicians of his day, he argued for justice for the working classes, fairness to women (and also the vote), and respect for the values of common American citizens. While other Americans hastened toward war, he held out, as had Thomas Jefferson almost exactly a century earlier, for peaceful means of resolving international conflict. With a commitment to principle that has been rare in American political history, Bryan even resigned his high office under Wilson when he felt the president's policies were needlessly pushing the country toward war with Germany. After he left Washington, Bryan turned his energies increasingly to the campaign against the teaching of biological evolution in the nation's schools. To his mind, this task was only an extension of earlier efforts to preserve the rights of common citizens (against the imperialism of the elite) and traditional American religion (against the encroaching naturalism of an alien moral system). Unlike Wilson, Bryan never lapsed into disillusionment when his projects were defeated. Yet, like Wilson, his public activity often amounted to a politics of revival. It was strong on moral fervor and impressive in its rhetorical power, but it was weak in practical strategy and deficient in political realism. As a result, his reforming urge spun him further and further away from practical political influence. Wilson's crusading zeal carried him to political disillusionment; Bryan's ended by making him politically irrelevant.

CIVIL RIGHTS AND THE NEW CHRISTIAN RIGHT

Though much more briefly, I suggest that the history played out by Woodrow Wilson and William Jennings Bryan has continued throughout our century. In recent years the two most important political causes with significant Christian elements have been the civil rights movement and the New Christian Right. From a Christian perspective both are laudable in several ways. Leaders of the civil rights movement, like the Reverend Martin Luther King, Jr., used Christian insight and the vocabulary of Scripture to push Americans beyond the racist hypocrisies of our history. Leaders of the New Christian Right, like the Reverend Jerry Falwell, have employed Christian motives to attack the palpable influence of atheistic secularism on our society. It is not necessary to equate these two movements—for partisans of one are often incapable of seeing any virtues in the other—in order to say that they have each contributed significantly as Christian movements to American life.

At the same time, for all their virtues, they have also shared the characteristic weaknesses of American Christian politics. In both, a talent for words races beyond political skill; it has been easier to be rhetorically fervent, to rouse the faithful to march or send in a check, than politically effective, to translate moral impulse into effective social change.

In both movements limited political goals have been confused with substantial structural reforms. The civil rights movement secured the legal protection of black citizens, yet legal protection of equal opportunity did not reverse black urban poverty or strengthen the imperiled black family. The New Christian Right seeks legislation permitting prayer in public schools, yet formal prayers in school will not restore lost standards of decency or offer serious help to families and churches in their effort to train spiritually the new generation.

In both movements fervent moral impulses have led leaders to make political alliances in order to achieve their goals. Yet in both cases political participation has led to a loss of clarity for Christian foundations, whether civil rights extended speciously to defend abortion-on-demand or conservative "traditional values" broadened to include a unqualified defense of free-market capitalism.

Finally, in both movements a legitimate appeal for reform has taken flight into conspiratorial nonsense. On the one hand, leaders of the civil rights movement are susceptible to the Marxist myth of manipulative class antagonism. On the other hand, leaders of the New Christian Right are susceptible to the native myth of a "Christian America" stolen away by the secular humanists. In both cases, the myths are not entirely false, but when they are transformed into universal theories, explaining everything that goes on in American politics and society, they take their place with the Bavarian Illuminati as delusions marring America's political history.

These comments, it is obvious, do not amount to a balanced judgment on either the civil rights movement or the New Christian Right. The point rather is to show that the experience of America's recent past repeats some of the strengths and weaknesses in our history. Today, as in the past, we see dedicated Christians putting themselves on the line for the values that define their existence personally. Today, as in the past, we see the significant benefit that the country derives from that activity. Today, as in the past, we also see characteristic problems arising from that activity.

SPRINGS OF ACTION

The mingled legacy of Christian political action—the presence in our history of conditions both to praise and to blame—calls for still more precise assessment. What explains, in other words, the particular goals to which American Christians have directed their political activity? What ideals of public life, or of the state, have guided believers in their action? How have Christians addressed questions of ends and means? How, that is, have they resolved the problem of finding strategies for political action that comport with the standards of their faith? And how have American Christians managed the delicate transition from general moral persuasion to organized political action?

The historical chapters in this book have shown that these more reflective questions do not loom large in American political history. It is far more characteristic of American Christians to act first and reflect later (if ever) than to engage in self-conscious consideration of their own activities.

This observation, however, is simply another way of drawing attention to what we have already noted about political action by American Christians. Such action is "Reformed," as defined in an earlier chapter. It moves directly from personal conviction to public program, assuming that what is morally good for the individual can and should be translated directly into something morally good for society. Christian political action in America has also been an extension of the revival. The prevailing characteristics of revival—its immediatism, ultraism, and perfectionism—create a peculiarly American style of "political evangelism" or "evangelistic politics." As we have observed, the "Reformed" assumption about the relation between individuals and society and the revivalistic style of political activity explain both successes and shortcomings of Christian political action. We have, in short, experienced the vices of our virtues.

In the last analysis, these historical circumstances are the explanation for the paradox seen so often in our history. Intense, all-or-nothing political action from Christian motives has led to a broad range of political achievements—more briefly, *without* fervor, no results. On the other hand, that kind of intense, all-or-nothing Christian political action has been marred by excess, disillusionment, unchristian tactics, and other problems—*with* fervor, ironic results.

Given such a history, it seems obvious that American Christians need to preserve the virtues of past activity, but also seek further insight. That insight is most needed when considering the nature of political action itself, the range of possible results from political action, and the relation of political action to the preservation of Christianity. Another way of approaching the same concern is to ask, What adjustments could aid political action by American Christians? What has been missing in our history that could improve both the political and the religious quality of public behavior?

THE WEAKNESSES OF OUR HISTORY

A first conclusion is that revivalism does not provide a comprehensive political style adequate for all purposes. When the techniques of revival have been brought to bear on political issues, considerable good has resulted. Political revivalists can spotlight issues, enlist volunteers, heighten moral dimensions, and present ideals. But the ultraism, immediatism, and perfectionism of revival do not contribute much to other essential aspects of the political task. Revivalism offers a poor model for working at complicated, deeply rooted, or contentious problems. It is much better at painting a vision of where society should be headed than at providing a blueprint for how to get there. It also serves more readily to call people to social engagement than to tell them how to negotiate with others who do not share their views. In sum, the strengths of revivalism as applied to politics are many, but revivalism by itself cannot offer a well-rounded political vision or do much to suggest a workable political strategy.

Weaknesses in the revivalistic approach to politics point to a more fundamental difficulty, which is the general absence in America of theological reflection on political questions. Christian political action in America characteristically occurs at the level of personal morality, rather than at the level of theology. Yet theological issues, whether recognized or not, do in fact lay the foundation for Christian political action. What is the relation between the nature of God and the human social order? Between the nature of humanity and the realm of the politically possible? Between the drama of fall and redemption and the struggle against social evil? Between the nature of the created order and the character of political institutions? Such questions rarely receive careful consideration when the insistent inner dynamic is always to action, always to speeding up the transition from intuited good to political goal.

Even our brief survey of American politics, however, shows that where there has been deeper reflection on such foundational theological questions, the political result is unusually favorable. James Madison pondered the nature of humanity—marked both by persistent selfishness and the potential for greatness—more seriously than did the professional clergymen of his day. It is therefore not surprising that the shape of the Constitution and the arguments of *The Federalist* reflect a more profound grasp of the ambiguous character of human beings than that displayed by most of the ministers and revivalists among Madison's contemporaries. The same may be said for Lincoln. While he pondered the *mysteries* of divine providence, preachers and religious writers in his generation blared forth their *certain knowledge* of God's plan for America. Is it any wonder, then, that ministerial commentary on the Civil War, distorted as it was by extreme partisanship, has vanished from sight, while Lincoln's second inaugural, from the pen of a man who never joined a church, remains alive as one of the most profound religious statements in all of American public life?

The history of Christian politics in America reveals the need for serious theological reflection at many points. The first requirement is simply for more of this kind of thought. But second, the quality of thought is also important. Madison and Lincoln were distinguished in their times not simply because they brooded on themes with theological implications; they were distinguished also because of the quality of their thought. They did not rest with easy, superficial truths, but penetrated further to the clash of opposites (humans as good and evil) and to the limits of human understanding (a good God ordaining the carnage of warfare). Madison and Lincoln would not have understood it this way, but in terms of our earlier discussion of approaches to culture, they were adding a "Lutheran" leaven to the "Reformed" lump otherwise the norm in America.

Third, if our political history has lacked a base of theological reflection, it has also lacked more direct religious consideration of the nature of politics itself. The point is not to call for a "Christian politics," for such a term is most frequently heard from partisans trying to dignify their own parochial positions with God-talk. The point is rather the need for Christian reflection on the contexts and constraints of political life. Reflection arising directly from Christian foundations is needed if we are to address the great underlying questions of political life: What may we expect of political effort? What, at its best, can it accomplish; what, at its worst, does it leave unaffected? How much can the state actually do to guarantee justice? How must the necessary functioning of government be balanced by the actions of families, churches, and economic organizations?

A few Americans have addressed themselves to such issues in our history. John Winthrop, the first governor of Puritan Massachusetts, was one leader who thought about these matters, and with great effect.[7] As Winthrop, from the foundation provided by Scripture and his religious tradition, pondered the situation of Puritans in England and New England, he concluded that government could accomplish much (it could establish economic and social order, and even aid the church) but only if the quality of governing was sound (ruling did not amount to a mechanical exertion of power but a self-giving altruism on the part of the ruler). As an active ruler, Winthrop was not perfect, but he still exhibited a faithfulness and realism in his political activities rare indeed in American history.

In the twentieth century the works of Reinhold Niebuhr represented a similar kind of deep brooding over the theological nature of political life. To take just one example, Niebuhr's book *Moral Man and Immoral Society* (1932) revived the sort of reflection on human nature that James Madison had practiced at the end of the eighteenth century. As Niebuhr saw the world through the lens of his Christian tradition, he scoffed at the idea that a simple optimism about human nature could adequately guide international relations. The path to social justice lay not through naive progressivism, not through a naive idealism, but through a chastened use of power. Conflict was inevitable, and no system of international relations would ever be effective if it dismissed this reality. Niebuhr's specific proposals have been praised and criticized since his day. They have also had a deep and far-ranging influence among Christians of many varieties and also among some nonbelievers. The reason is that his political vision rested on a firm, disciplined, and profound theological foundation.

A final deficiency in American political history goes beyond the lack of theological reflection on political theory to the lack of theological reflection on political practice. The two are related, for careful Christian consideration of politics as such (as with Winthrop and Niebuhr) usually points to the necessity in the political process of negotiation, give-and-take, and (within limits) compromise. If the God who made all human beings also made the public sphere and ordained government to promote justice for all, then it is apparent that God has given all men and women a stake in politics. This being so, no impulse of Christian morality, regardless how correct on its own terms, should ever negate the God-given privilege of all people to hold a place in the political sun. Even when pursuing political goals consistent with Christian thinking, believers have no excuse for disregarding the humanity and the God-ordained dignity of the other participants in the political process. These truisms point to the need for considerable sophistication in political tactics. The means used in politics must not contradict the noble goals of Christian political action.

The crusade against slavery offers one of the outstanding examples in American history of the need for a better political strategy. When William Lloyd Garrison and his allies pursued abolition revivalistically in the 1830s and early 1840s, the result was disarray and political ineffectiveness. Only when the force of events succeeded in drawing together the energies of radical abolitionists with those of "free-soilers" (who wanted blacks kept out of the territories), political moderates like Lincoln (who as late as 1862 was asking black leaders to take freed slaves to Africa), and moderate abolitionists (who could tolerate gradual emancipation) did slavery come to an end. Sobering words addressed by Harriet Beecher Stowe to Garrison are a continuing caution against political ultraism: "Is there but one true anti-slavery church," she asked, "and all the rest infidels?"[8]

An instructive contrast to American patterns can be found in the fight against slavery in England as directed by William Wilberforce.[9] Wilberforce, an evangelical member of the Church of England who had gone into Parliament as a young man, was every bit as opposed to slavery as Garrison was. Even more than Garrison, Wilberforce was convinced that standard Christian teaching was the proper platform from which to launch and sustain the attack on slavery.

What most distinguished Wilberforce's long campaign against slavery—which began in 1787 and did not come to an end until the year of his death, 1833, when Parliament outlawed slavery in all British possessions—was its concern for strategy. Wilberforce was both persistent and patient. He was willing year after year to submit legislation to Parliament aimed at rolling back now one, now another feature of the slave system, even when such legislation met with persistent opposition. Through both triumphs and defeats, Wilberforce attended to painstaking political details on many levels—gathering what we would today call "hard data from the field" in support of his proposed legislation, regularly reviewing how his other political activities affected the fight against slavery, carefully mending his fences with the powerful leaders of Parliament, going out of his way to win over opponents and to show how their best interests would be served by the abolition of slavery. Wilberforce could also accept halfway measures, as for example when he voted in 1806 to continue slavery itself as a concession necessary for winning Parliament's abolition of the slave trade. But in so doing he was only exercising his judgment about which tactics would best lead to his goal. One should not praise Wilberforce excessively, for he too made political blunders. Yet despite weaknesses, his career remains a helpful indication of how shrewd political strategy contributed to ultimate success.

In sum, the characteristic deficiencies of political action by American Christians are not inconsiderable. At the same time, they are consistent with the more general Christian positions that have prevailed throughout the history of the United States. The modification of revivalistic

10. The Bible and Politics

Political action that would be Christian must draw strength from the Scriptures. To be sure, many other resources are necessary for properly Christian political behavior. From the side of religion, it is necessary to make use of the riches of Christian tradition, the special insights of ministers, priests, and bishops, and the inner promptings of the Spirit. Christian political action should also be based on the great political wisdom—both theoretical and practical—to be found among those indifferent, or even hostile, to Christianity. But especially in America, where appeal to the language of the Bible is so much a part of the political tradition, we will never have *Christian* political action if we do not have *biblical* political action.[1]

ROADBLOCKS

Immediately, however, two difficulties appear. The first is practical and historical. Has not the political use of the Bible in America amounted to a weary parade of misapplication, text mongering, self-serving interpretation, and (in general) abuse of Scripture? The second difficulty is theoretical and theological. Even if we think the Bible is a revelation from God, how in fact do we move from its pages, from cultures very different from our own, to our world today? Both of these problems are serious ones that cannot be lightly dismissed.

In the first instance, a recurring, if inadequately studied, feature of American history is the way that Christians have reflexively turned to the Bible for political purposes. Motives have often been laudable, especially a desire for the word of God to speak to the needs of the moment. And the Scriptures have indeed played a powerful role at many critical moments of our history. Thus, biblical phrases have often been spoken publicly during the nation's great crises—social, economic, and especially military. Ministers and lay leaders alike have turned to

Scripture in the hour of national need, and from it they have taken words of comfort, encouragement, and fortitude.

By the same token, however, the national use of the Bible has frequently had unfortunate results. Too often the introduction of Scripture has meant the end of political discourse and the beginning of rhetorical excoriation, the end of interchange and the beginning of strife. In such cases, as from pulpits North and South during the Civil War, the Bible functions merely as a way of heightening the dignity, weight, and force of a faction's own political positions, whether or not these have anything to do with the essential themes of Scripture. From the standpoint of religion, this way of employing the Bible is simply a disaster: Scripture no longer speaks to us; rather, we exploit it to say what we want to say.

Unfortunately, our history is filled with examples of such abuse. There was the Connecticut Congregationalist who in 1773 preached a sermon on the virtues of home rule and the danger of government from afar based on Exodus 1:8 ("Now there arose up a new king over Egypt, which knew not Joseph," KJV).[2] The next year a Presbyterian patriot was just as creative with his use of Colossians 2:21 ("Touch not; taste not; handle not," KJV) for a *Sermon on Tea.*[3] Early in the Civil War a Southerner transformed a prayer of King Solomon into a commentary on the crisis of his day. The text was 2 Chronicles 6:34–35; from it came this message: "Eleven tribes sought to go forth in peace from the house of political bondage, but the heart of our modern Pharaoh is hardened, that he will not let Israel go."[4] Similar abuses of the Bible have attended most of our major national crises and many of our influential political crusades.

The historical incidents traced in this book also offer a cautionary word about the abuse of Scripture. On the basis of proof-texting from the Old Testament, Southern Christians were able to construct a broad defense of slavery. Some Northerners, like William Lloyd Garrison, seemed half-convinced that the Southerners were correct and so stopped taking the Bible so seriously. More typically, Northern Bible readers tried to present a countervailing set of isolated texts, or they mumbled vaguely about how "the spirit of the Bible" opposed slavery. The second strategy did in fact point in a helpful direction, but Northerners usually employed it only when pressed to do so by their Southern opponents. Northerners really were not searching for a more comprehensive use of the Bible but were being forced out of their preferred approach to the Scriptures as a quarry of texts by the quantity of similar material already hewn by Southerners from the same source.

Difficulties were less complicated in the campaign against drink, but they were no less obvious. No matter what the intellectual gymnastics of ardent prohibitionists, the Bible really does say that the patriarchs, the prophets, Jesus, and his disciples drank fermented beverages. It may have been inconvenient for the cause—and so an occasion for trying to scurry around the transparent meaning of such passages—but there it was. The Bible, which was exalted as the supreme authority by most temperance advocates, did not reinforce their political conclusion clearly enough, so it had to be amended.

Those who would put the Bible to use politically must, therefore, admit that the precedents are not particularly encouraging. The word of God consistently appears to take on the political shading of those who attempt to put it to use.

Religious issues pose even more difficulties than we see in the history of the Bible's political abuse. Questions about the interpretation of the Bible have exercised the minds of many great thinkers, through many lifetimes of work. Yet using the Bible responsibly is not merely the task of professional Bible scholars and theologians. It is, in fact, too important a matter to be left to the professionals. Naive Bible thumping is not the answer, but neither is a timorous fear of trying to hear the Bible in our current situation. The effort to find the meaning of the Bible for politics is an effort that must be open to correction and rebuke, but it is also an effort of concern to all Christian at all times.

In the pages that follow I propose a series of steps that end with the employment of the Bible for contemporary political action. I may misunderstand the Bible, the nature of politics, or the relationship between biblical and political realities; still, I hope that these proposals about how to bring Scripture into play for political action can stimulate more thoughtful reflection in others, so that in their turn they may make strides toward a better understanding of the Bible, a more responsible Christian approach to politics, and an improved course of Christian political action.

THE BIBLE FIRST FOR ITSELF

The first, and most important, principle for putting the Bible to use in politics must be to focus on the Bible itself. This might seem a detour to the goal of a politically relevant Scripture, but it is in fact the most direct route to that goal. A recovery of the Bible for politics must begin with a recovery of the Bible for itself.

What is most obvious about the Bible, however, is that it is not primarily a book about politics, or science, or psychology, or any other field. Before everything else, the Bible is the story of salvation, the record of how God has reached down to an undeserving humanity in order to restore communion with himself. This is the message of the Bible. In the words of Jesus as recorded in the Gospel of John, "The scriptures . . . bear witness to me"; the things that were written of Jesus were recorded "that you may believe that Jesus is the Christ, the Son of God, and that believing you may have life in his name" (John 5:39; 20:31). The New Testament epistles proclaim the same message, as in 2 Timothy 3:15, where it is claimed that "the sacred writings . . . are able to instruct you for salvation through faith in Christ Jesus." Such statements are doubly important since they refer primarily to the Scriptures of the Old Testament even before those of the New. In the Bible's own words, then, the Bible is about reconciliation with God.

This is also the conclusion drawn by the leaders of the Protestant Reformation, especially those branches of Protestantism that made up the prehistory of America's predominant faiths. "Holy Scripture," as the fifth of the Church of England's Thirty-nine Articles from 1563 had it, "containeth all things necessary to salvation." Or in the words of the Westminster Confession of 1646, "The light of nature, and the works of creation and providence . . . are not sufficient to give that knowledge of God, and of his will, which is necessary unto salvation; therefore it pleased the Lord . . . to reveal himself, and to declare that his will unto his Church; and afterward . . . to commit the same wholly unto writing; which maketh the holy Scripture to be most necessary."[5]

Having recognized the centrality of salvation in Scripture, we must hasten to note that in the Bible "salvation" does not mean simply "conversion" (the turning to God) but also "holiness" (the living to God). Salvation, thus, is both otherworldly (a rescue for eternity) and also intensely this-worldly (a rescue for the present). And so although the central message of the Bible is the story of how sinners in need of God can come to him, this message speaks to all other spheres of life. The Bible begins with the encounter between the divine and the human, but ends by speaking to all relationships that God has or-dained—individuals with each other, people gathered in groups to other groups, and human beings as a whole in relation to their environ-ment. The message of the Bible does not speak with equal directness to every sphere of our lives, yet because its message of salvation is so central to human existence, and because it is so multifaceted, the Bible affects every feature, every dimension, of our lives, including the political.

Care is necessary to follow out the Bible's implications for politics, since political circumstances change in ways that basic spiritual matters do not. Christian in fact hold that the basic human realities to which the Bible speaks are everywhere the same: the need to repent and believe the gospel, the responsibility to treat our neighbors as ourselves, the centrality of the church in God's purposes, the foundational character of family, work, and government as ordinances created by God. At the same time, few would deny that conditions of human existence vary significantly from place to place and time to time. The conditions of twentieth-century America, for instance, are considerably altered from the conditions in which King David or the Apostle Paul lived. We now live in communities very different from the relatively closed, face-to-face communities of the ancient world. Our awareness of world affairs is much greater than it was in the biblical age. Most of us are much more insulated from the experience of death and dying than those of the biblical generations. Our conceptions of science, music, and art are different, as are our means of communication, our methods of political organization, our expectations for the economy. In other words, the

Bible's central message may be the same now as it always was, but the world in which we hear that message has changed considerably from the world in which it was first heard.

Given this change of circumstances, we will misapply Scripture if we act as if it were a simple matter to apply its teachings directly to modern politics. The key to using the Bible fruitfully for politics is to remember its character, to recall that it speaks first to men and women in their relationship with God. But then it is appropriate to go further and affirm that although the Bible speaks comprehensively to human beings in their relationships with each other, its general message about God and the human condition is an orienting message. It does not offer a detailed blueprint for action today, but it does offer a framework for a plan of action.

THE BIBLE PUT TO USE POLITICALLY

If we understand the Scriptures in this way, how should we bring the Bible into play for political action today? The following injunctions suggest a way. They are attempts to recognize both the essential character of Scripture and its capacity to speak to modern situations.

(1) The most important matter is to aim at being biblical Christian above all else. Given the many demands upon our loyalties, from within our own natures and from the society in which we live, it is no easy matter to succeed at such a goal. Yet it is the starting point for a genuinely Christian political action. To aim at being a biblical Christian above all else means that self-identity must come from Christian faith and not from American citizenship. It means that we are first Christians, and only then capitalists, socialists, or defenders of a mixed economy. It means that we will be Christian who happen to be Republicans or Democrats, rather than Democrats or Republicans who happen to be Christians. The faith will loom larger than support for social security, welfare reform, farmer relief, anti-abortion legislation, or a nuclear freeze. It is unlikely that anyone can fully succeed in setting so rigorously the demands of the faith before other allegiances, but it is nonetheless the place to begin.

(2) A second goal is to interpret the Bible with respect to its own

integrity. Since the key to the abuse of the Bible is the abuse of its interpretation, it is necessary to take scrupulous care in bringing the Scriptures to bear on public life. Without the Bible's general guidelines, Christians are simply at sea. But they may be in even more desperate straits if the impetus to gain biblical support for a political position leads to wanton proof-texting, to wrenching of passages away from their proper context, and to illogical application of biblical themes.

The following two examples can suggest the problems of ideological interpretation. Debates over welfare have sometimes drawn attention to a phrase from Jesus recorded in the story of the woman who anointed his head with an expensive ointment. When the disciples criticized the woman for wasting money, Jesus responded, "You always have the poor with you, but you will not always have me" (Matt. 26:11). A casual misapplication of that phrase might be used to support the conclusion that care for the poor is somehow a marginal social priority for Christians. Something quite different emerges, however, when the Old Testament source of Jesus' statement is brought into the picture, for there we read, "The poor will never cease out of the land; therefore I command you, You shall open wide your hand to your brother, to the needy and to the poor, in the land" (Deut. 15:11). Assuming, then, that Jesus knew the context of the passage from Deuteronomy, our conclusion about his words might well be that he was speaking primarily about his own role in God's economy of salvation and not to restrain concern for the poor.

In a similar manner, the words of 2 Chronicles 7:14 are sometimes applied to the United States ("If my people who are called by my name humble themselves, and pray and seek my face, and turn from their wicked ways, then I will hear from heaven and will forgive their sin and heal their land"). This passage clearly speaks to the relationship between private lives and public well-being, yet closer attention to the text shows that "my people" can only apply to the Old Testament Israelites to whom God had made special covenantal promises. A consistently Christian reading of the Bible would therefore conclude that application of this text in the modern world must focus not on modern nations, to which God has made no special promises, but to his Church, which exists in a dispersed state throughout most of the world.

In sum, we need to go much further than simply the random alignment of biblical texts with contemporary situations. The task, rather, is intelligent application of biblical passages, understood in the terms of their own context, to carefully analyzed situations in the present.

(3) Political action consistent with biblical faith will tend to focus on broad themes of Scripture that inform both the Old and New Testaments. The most general themes of the Bible, the convictions shared by patriarchs and prophets, by Jesus and his disciples, provide the foundational insights for politics, as for all other spheres of life. These themes draw us to the heart of Scripture, to its story of salvation, to God's generous gift of general mercy to all humanity, and to his specific challenge to the Church of living out the values of his kingdom. (It is worth recording in passing that a valuable point of dialogue between Christians and Jews arises from a comparison of politically relevant themes that Jews derive from the Hebrew Scriptures and later rabbinic reflection on those Scriptures and politically relevant themes that Christian find in reading the New Testament with the Hebrew Scriptures.)

The journey is long from the Bible's general themes and its story of salvation to questions of political decision today. But to move from broad themes of Scripture to their specific application is nonetheless one way of reducing the likelihood that biblical passages will be used for parochial, ideological, or factional purposes.

(4) In principle, proper reasoning from the Bible leads to conclusions that are harmonious with proper reasoning from the nature of the political process. Viewed theologically, this is only an affirmation that God's special revelation in Scripture and his general revelation to the hearts and minds of all people are of a piece, since God himself is one. Christian should therefore look for harmony between political conclusions drawn from the Bible and political wisdom drawn from the fund of human learning and practice.

Actual practice, of course, falls far short of the ideal; the potential harmony may be lost in many ways. Believers can misinterpret the Bible. Conclusions drawn from political experience and political reflection may be skewed because of prejudice or incomplete knowledge.

Political reasoning appropriate to one set of circumstances may not translate easily into another set of circumstances. In addition, Christians may make mistakes in bringing together their interpretations of the Bible and their analyses of political circumstances. And there are yet more places where disharmony seems to arise between reasoning from Scripture and reasoning from political life. But even to mention these possibilities suggests something of the nature of the task.

It is even the case that in certain modern situations, two contrasting political positions may both have reasonably strong claims to be "biblical" positions. This has happened, for instance, in some recent debates over America's defense posture. Biblical imperatives toward maintaining peace are very strong. But the Bible also speaks clearly about the need for rulers to defend the property and traditions of their people (thus seeming to justify a strong national defense, including nuclear armament in a nuclear age) and about the virtues of taking risks, even to the point of turning the other cheek, to secure peace (thus seeming to justify vigorous efforts at reducing nuclear arms). The biblical principles are, as such, not necessarily incompatible, but on any one piece of legislation it is conceivable that a vote for and a vote against may both arise from a process of "biblical reasoning."

This does not mean that the Bible may mean simply anything at all. It suggests, rather, that the fixed character of the Bible's central themes provides a framework, a set of boundaries, within which to work out Christian positions on political issues. These themes do not usually offer a specific plan for legislation or a specific series of guidelines specifying proper political actions in all times and places.

(5) Finally, the possibility of contrasting "biblical positions" on controverted modern issues points up the positive value, within a Christian frame of reference, of political negotiations, discussion, and compromise. If we reason from general orienting principles to specific cases, we are bound to benefit from sympathetic efforts to understand alternative points of view—both from Christians (with whom we might differ on how to interpret biblical themes) and from nonbelievers (to whom God has given a full measure of general political wisdom). With such a view, it is possible to have a positive estimation of the give-and-take of the political world. That world is not an amoral

boxing ring where the Christian's only duty is to defend a tightly defined position, but a marketplace provided by God. In such a marketplace, some proposals and procedures will still be morally or spiritually abhorrent. But that will not destroy the educational potential of the marketplace, where the Christian can expect, in the process of negotiation and dialogue, to learn a great deal from other participants (who, like the Christian, bear the image of God) and especially from other Christians (who are also trying to act in accord with God's revealed will). We may in fact be so bold as to expect to learn as much from those who oppose us on specific political issues as from those who share our position.

The kind of approach to political action that I have sketched here makes much of the Bible's general themes. Such an emphasis naturally raises the question of what those themes might look like.

"BIBLICAL" POLITICS

I therefore suggest two themes as examples of general biblical positions. In proposing these themes, it is entirely possible that I have misread the biblical story or misunderstood its relevance to politics. Still, ordering principles for a genuinely Christian political action will probably be characterized by some of the same features of generality and applicability that I suggest here.

First, because God is supremely just and equitable in his dealings with humanity, the structures of government and the capacity for politics that God communicated to human beings should have as their purpose justice and equity. The likelihood that this is an important theme for political application is heightened by the way that it appears in many biblical contexts. Rulers in the Mosaic dispensation were told, "You shall not pervert justice; you shall not show partiality; and you shall not take a bribe, for a bribe blinds the eyes of the wise and subverts the cause of the righteous. Justice, and only justice, you shall follow" (Deut. 16:19–20). King David was singled out for praise because he "administered justice and equity to all his people" (2 Sam. 8:15). Later in Israel's history, the prophets raged at the misapplication of justice. The political fatcats of Israel were ordered to "hate evil, and love good, and establish justice in the gate [the place of adjudicating disputes]" (Amos 5:15), and the leaders of Judah were chastised because "no one enters suit justly, no one goes to law honestly, they rely on empty pleas, they speak lies, they conceive mischief and bring forth iniquity" (Isa. 59:4). A similar concern for justice is present in the New Testament, where, for example, the Apostle Paul urges masters to "treat your slaves justly and fairly, knowing that you also have a Master in heaven" (Col. 4:1). Many of the parables of Jesus revolve around the just or unjust dealings of rulers (e.g., Matt. 18:23–35), as do many of his ethical injunctions (Matt. 23:4).

In short, the Bible as a whole seems to call us to look on ruling in relation to the creation or preservation of public justice, not in relation to the raw exercise of power or the pursuit of self-interest. Such a call is still quite general, but it could exert a critical influence on the attitudes of Christians to the structures of government.

Second, it is perhaps the most important teaching of the Bible that God, the all-powerful, revealed himself to humanity most clearly and most fully in his powerlessness. Jesus, the divine Son of God, fulfilled his role most completely on the cross, in order to rescue human beings rendered helpless by their guilt before God. If such a theme has a political corollary, it must be that one of the most important tasks of the political order, as a God-given sphere of creation, is to care especially for the powerless, the marginal, and the oppressed. If the New Testament account is correct that "while we were yet helpless, at the right time Christ died for the ungodly" (Rom. 5:6), and if the central themes of the Bible are relevant to the central themes of a Christian politics, then we should expect that government would exercise special concern for those who are without strength in the social order.

This conclusion rests on much more than a general process of theological reasoning, for the Bible from cover to cover is filled with exhortations to that same end. The law of Moses included many injunctions, general and specific, to the effect that "you shall not pervert the justice due to your poor in his suit" (Exod. 23:6). The psalmists record the words of God directed to the same end, as in 82:3, "Give justice to the weak and the fatherless; maintain the right of the afflicted and the destitute." The prophets urged their listeners constantly to "learn to do good; seek justice, correct oppression; defend the fatherless, plead for the widow" (Isa. 1:17). Jesus claimed to be sent especially "to preach good news to the poor . . . to proclaim release to the captives and recovering of sight to the blind, to set at liberty those who are oppressed, to proclaim the acceptable year of the Lord" (Luke 4:18–19). Those who, like Zaccheus, came to Jesus often turned immediately to assist the poor (Luke 19:8). And the apostles often urged the ones to whom they spoke to "remember the poor" (Gal. 2:10). The parade of biblical texts could go on and on, but enough has been said to suggest how much the Scriptures stress the need to care for the powerless.

Simply to note this biblical theme does not provide either a political strategy or a political agenda. To know that God wants his people to make special efforts on behalf of the socially marginal does not, for most questions, tell us in twentieth-century America exactly how we are to go about that task. Yet to the extent that God is to be obeyed in the political process, as in the realm of private spirituality, to that extent political goals and purposes must include the divinely sanctioned concern for those who are without money, power, and prestige in this world.

To be sure, significant question remains about means to the end. We may agree, for example, on the need to provide for the marginalized poor, but disagree on whether the provision should best come directly through welfare transfers or indirectly through incentives to industry for the creation of new jobs and the training of the chronically unemployed. We may be in favor of a higher minimum wage out of concern for providing more adequately for those at the lowest end of the employment ladder, or we may oppose a higher minimum wage out of fear that it would decrease opportunities for those who have no employment. It may not be possible to reach one, widely shared "biblical platform" on such matters. Moreover, conflict over means will definitely occur among those, Christians and nonbelievers, who operate from relatively the same orienting principles. But if we seek greater clarity by thinking through the relationship of means and ends, we will be less likely to regard conflicts over means as if these were conflicts over first-level religious loyalties. A sense of proportion will preserve us from the error of the ardent prohibitionists who regarded every argument against prohibition as an assault on the faith, or from the mistake of the Southerners who looked at all attacks on slavery as the product of moral corruption in the North.

A sensitivity to means and ends does not mean, however, that all conflicts can be relativized. Some political disputes do concern first principles. These deserve to be, and often have been, the most seriously contested ones in the political arena. In American history the deepest divide over the question of personhood under God occurred on the issue of slavery. It is no surprise, then, that it took our bloodiest internal conflict to resolve the issue. The modern debate over abortion has the potential for becoming an issue of comparable conflict. That conflict is very basic because it pits against each other contrasting positions deeply rooted in overarching views of human nature, between, that is, those (like myself) who insist upon legal protection for the least significant members of society, even the silent unborn, and those who hold that the individual right to privacy is a higher value than protection for the weak. Though this contemporary standoff is complicated by other factors (e.g., antiabortionists who do not show much concern for other classes of the powerless, or prochoice advocates who stand up for others without a voice in our society); still, conflict penetrates to profound levels of commitment on this issue.

BIBLICAL MEANS TO BIBLICAL ENDS

A "biblical politics," in short, will be controlled by central biblical themes, by the critical elements in the history of salvation. But it will also be carried out with attention to the political process itself. Christians need much help in meeting the opportunities and the obligations of faithful political life. But even here, the Bible itself points to several general suggestions for carrying on political action that would be faithful to its central themes.

The first such suggestion is to distrust the "obvious" meaning of the Bible if such a meaning works mostly to support my interests, my power, or my economic stake in a particular situation. The prophet Jeremiah reminded the people of his day that "the heart is deceitful above all things, and desperately corrupt" (17:9). It is the same today.

Christians regard themselves not as perfect people but as forgiven people. They must recognize their continuing capacity to deceive themselves. They must not forget that it is possible to employ the Bible politically for selfish purposes as well as to advance justice.

Second, it is well to remember that the political arena belongs to all, not just to Christians, and not just to right-thinking Christians (i.e, those who agree with me). Causes that we think are in line with the central themes of Christianity should be prosecuted vigorously, but never so vigorously as to transform opponents into nonbeings. Political opponents remain fully dignified human beings made in the image of God, fully worthy people for whom Christ died. Their dignity and worth cannot be sacrificed in order for us to gain a political goal.

Third, it is very important for believers to examine alternatives to their political positions, especially those proposed by other Christians, but also from the world as a whole. The possession of Christian faith does not guarantee clear reasoning about a current political question, nor does it guarantee an ability to align biblical reasoning appropriately with contemporary analysis. At all times, and in all ways, we continue to need all the help we can get.

Fourth, Christian political action must be responsible. It deserves to be more cautious than it has often been in American history. At the same time, Christian political action remains a crying necessity. The needs of our day that may be addressed politically are immense. Christians, who know something of the one who made the world and all that it contains, dare not abandon that world to itself. Cautious, responsible, nuanced, self-critical political action, yes; but unhesitating political action nonetheless.

In this chapter we have only scratched the surface of what could be said about the employment of the Bible for a better form of Christian political action. It is a subject of immense dimensions and utmost practicality. Yet a concentrated effort to use the Bible more, and more consistently, is a great necessity. The need to put the Bible to use politically, and to do so more responsibly, is an urgent need, even in a land where the Bible is well known, well read, and indeed no stranger to the public arena.

It is easy to despair about understanding and making use of the Bible, especially in light of intense disagreements over its nature and meanings. It is also easy to despair about putting the Bible fruitfully to use in politics, given the many pitfalls along the way from a grasp of its pages to its faithful employment in the complicated arena of modern politics. It is nonetheless what Christians must do. The Bible contains the words of life. Just as they bring light into the darkness of our own lives, so they have a light to shed on the political darkness of our age.

11. The Challenge Today

The challenge of Christian politics must always be two-sided. The first side is the challenge to understand the Christian faith in such a way as to perceive its relevance for the political arena. The second is the challenge to grasp the realities of public life in such a way as to effectively apply Christian reasoning. The goal of Christian politics is equally daunting, nothing less than to promote the good of society while preserving the integrity of the faith.

APPRECIATING THE PAST

An examination of history provides solid reason for appreciating "America's Christian heritage." Taken in the qualified and restricted sense of that phrase, it is possible for contemporary believers to be deeply grateful for the quantity and the quality of Christian political behavior in our history. If there are serious flaws in that history (and there are), that is no reason to dismiss our predecessors. It is also no reason for entertaining the delusion that we, in our enlightenment, are not as susceptible to blunders of thought and practice as those in the past.

On the contrary, responsible Christian politics in our current situation must build upon the virtues of the past. Of first importance is to prize that which is unambiguously positive. James Madison's reflections on the political implications of the human condition, Abraham Lincoln's pregnant brooding on the mysteries of divine providence, even Thomas Jefferson's persistent efforts to govern without recourse to war—these are only some of the rich gifts to be simply appropriated from the American past.

There are also significant positive benefits to be gained from predecessors more like ourselves with their flaws of moral capacity and failures of political savvy. If we think that we are more realistic than

Charles Finney about the complexity of implementing moral change in society, we dare not be less ardent than he in demonstrating the need for holiness in a Christian's public as well as private life. If we realize the value of political negotiation more clearly than William Lloyd Garrison, we must still admire his courage in challenging the political complacency of his generation. If we lower our sights from the millennial visions of Theodore Dwight Weld, we would still do well to imitate his energy in pursuit of political righteousness. If we abandon the mechanistic social theory that drove Neal Dow in his crusade against drink, we owe it to his memory to be no less concerned about the suffering brought on by overindulgence. If we see more readily the dangers of single-issue electioneering than the opponents of Thomas Jefferson, we can yet admire them for understanding that political choices shape the character of a civilization. If we consider ourselves less captive to simple partisanship than the Christian advocates of the Union or the Confederacy during the Civil War, it would be well if we showed their determination to include contemporary political considerations in the orbit of Christian concern. From such predecessors the proper conclusion is that we need *better* activism, not an end to activism. The ultraism, immediatism, and perfectionism of America's revival tradition are flawed political instruments, but they still contain much to admire.

By the same token, the "Reformed" assumptions that have dominated American political life could be enriched by other religious perspectives. I have suggested that a "Lutheran" contribution would be especially in order, particularly to show the complexity involved in moving from private moral vision to corporate public policy, or to recall the danger of justifying the self precisely at that moment when the Christian is most actively laboring for God. Signal elements from "Catholic" or "Anabaptist" approaches to culture no doubt also have much of value to contribute in America. Yet the truth of these assertions should not blind us to the achievements of the "Reformed" perspective. The engine of "Reformed" political action has sometimes run out of control by confusing partisan political imperatives with the faith. It has sometimes overreached itself by acting as if the accomplishment of a political goal would bring on the millennium. But it has also done too much good, both religiously and politically, to be lightly cast aside. For worse, but also for better, America's Christian heritage rests on a "Reformed" foundation.

In short, it would be foolish as American Christians at the end of the twentieth century to deny that we are what we are. The millennial pretensions of our Christian predecessors should be no cause for this generation to lapse into cynicism or despair. To be sure, the task now is not to propose a new utopianism, to figure out another scheme to bring in the millennium; the task is instead to take advantage of work that has been done, to minimize the damage it has wrought, and to go on.

BENEFITS OF THEOLOGICAL REFLECTION

In seeking to build upon what has been done, we must begin with more and better theological reflection. "Theological reflection," however, sounds too highbrow; all it really means is thinking about what the existence of God and the truths of Christianity mean for political life, and then thinking about how such truths may be put to use. The more of such thinking, the better. It needs to come from academic theologians and Bible scholars using specialized vocabularies and drawing on extensive research, from preachers trying to enlighten their congregations, from sociologists and political scientists scouting out religiously sensitive aspects of the current scene, from church historians attempting to clarify the lessons of the past, from laypeople energetically reading the Scriptures and exploring the heritages of their churches in order to discover resources for the needs of the hour. Of special value, as I have suggested several times, will be theological reflection on the Christian themes that constitute the deep background for public life, and in addition, more specific reflection on the nature of government as ordained by God and on the proper methods of political action.

But what would such theological reflection yield? There is no mystery about the answer, at least in its general outlines, since theological reflection on the political situation today will almost certainly bring forth the same kind of conclusions that have appeared earlier in the history of the Church. What Augustine attempted when considering the meaning of the fall of Rome in the early fifth century; Thomas Aquinas in considering the practical Christian implications of trade, military service, and many other vexing issues in the thirteenth century; the Protestant Reformers of the sixteenth century in asking how a renewed appreciation for the Scriptures should affect the organizing of society; the Puritans of the seventeenth century in wondering how far to carry opposition to the king of England; popes in the nineteenth and twentieth centuries in seeking to guide Catholics in responding to modern industrial life—these are the sorts of things that must be discovered in our own day.

Others will provide different agendas, but I would hope that something like the following might come from a fuller exploration of Christian themes relevant to political quetions:

(1) Most simply, but also most importantly, I would hope for a wider recognition that deeper probing into the central Christian truths will enrich political life, as well as every other aspect of existence. To really know more of God—the mysteries of the divine Trinity, the ways of God with the material creation, the revelation of his will concerning life in society, the loving habits of his heart toward humanity—should be the controlling purpose of the Christian's life. From such reflection political benefit will not be automatic, but without such reflection there can be no purification of Christian political action.

(2) More intense theological reflection might also provide needed balance for understanding the political process, ourselves as political actors, and the church as a force in political life. If one of the characteristic flaws of American Christian politics is loss of balance, we need to learn about how balance may be retained. We need, that is, to know how better to combine energetic political pursuit of what is good for society with painstaking respect for those who would oppose our political purposes. We need to display boldness in political advocacy for what, under God, we have come to consider the right, even as we examine ourselves for any drift into self-righteousness. It would also be well to see more clearly how the church may participate in the shaping of a culture to the glory of God while simultaneously acting as a rebuke and counterweight to the sinful structures of this world.[1]

To understand the need for this kind of balance and, even more, actually to practice it, is one of the products of theological reflection in its fullest sense.

(3) It is also possible that a more reflective approach to Christian political theory may lead to more responsible Christian political action. Too often "Christian politics" is a smokescreen obscuring self-seeking efforts to retain power, wealth, or influence. A genuine Christian politics should lead more directly to the points at which others are suffering oppression or injustice. The practice of politics as self-interest is deeply ingrained in twentieth-century America. But if the followers of Christ, who "emptied himself" and took "the form of a servant" (Phil. 2:7), cannot break loose from the constraints of egotistic politics, who can?

A more responsible political action will also flow from more persistent theological reflection if it makes us more sensitive critics of contemporary political philosophies. In the current scene, we have a few carefully articulated positions from the Left, several alternative positions from the Right (a proportion reversing that of two decades ago), and a mass of intuitive political reasoning from various points along the pragmatic Center. Better theological reasoning should make us sharper critics, better able to see through pretense and self-justification, but also better able to appropriate genuinely moral insight and carefully reasoned argument wherever they are found. Christians who take seriously the belief that all people are made in God's image, that God ordained political life along with the other spheres of existence, and that God bestows freely on all people a general capacity for responsible thought should expect to find assistance in many surprising places.

(4) Finally, theological reflection should also aid us in the momentously important task of discriminating between the gospel itself and Christian activity attempting to live out the gospel. The Christian message transcends all political systems, all specificities of governmental structure, all individual political actions or decisions. Put more accurately, the message of the gospel is potentially embedded in all systems, governments, and actions; it is nowhere not at home. By its very universal character, Christianity offers compelling pointers for a more wholesome politics in every locale. Yet, it is still of vital importance

not to confuse the universal Christian message itself with its application in specific times and places. The gospel can work powerfully in every political situation, but only if the gospel is not absorbed by any one political situation. Christian political action must grow out of Christianity, but Christianity must never be exhausted by political action. As obvious as such statements seem in the abstract, they touch the most practical conclusions to be drawn from theological reflection on the political process.

CHRISTIAN POLITICS AND CHRISTIAN LIFE

To put matters most simply, a Christian politics alive to the faith and dedicated to the good of the public will reflect the general realities of Christian life. Christians, who believe in the potential goodness of the world (because made by God), are able to work wholeheartedly for improvement here and now. Christians, who realize the final incompleteness of this world (because not yet perfected by God), are also able to cope with failure, and even with success, in the here and now. What is true in general is true as well for politics.

Our historical sketches have recorded some of the successes and failures of Christian political action in American history. Were we to expand our history beyond politics, we would find the same range of failures and successes in other facets of American life. The crucial thing for considering political life—as it would be in those other spheres—is how much good has been done in the name of Christ but also how far short we fall of the Way he pioneered.

As it was appropriate in the Introduction to cite the words of Abraham Lincoln, the American who reflected most profoundly on Christian dimensions of our political life, so it is appropriate to conclude with words from the authority that was a constant object of Lincoln's reflection. In the words of Scripture we encounter the dialectic of human responsibility and divine grace proposed by the Apostle Paul, a dialectic as relevant for politics as for anything else: "Work out your own salvation with fear and trembling; for God is at work in you, both to will and work for his good pleasure" (Phil. 2:12–13). It is as if in the next election, the next confrontation in the legislature, the next battle before the courts, the next opportunity to mobilize in a great social crisis everything, and nothing, depended on us.

In Scripture we find as well the even more intense dialectic of Jesus. It was Jesus who, in effect, reminded his followers of the peril of political action with the words, "What good is it for a man to gain the whole world, yet forfeit his soul?"[2] But it was also Jesus who gave to his disciples "new" commandments ("Render therefore to Caesar the things that are Caesar's"; "You shall love your neighbor as yourself"; "As you did to one of the least of these my brethren, you did it to me"). And then, in an imperative for political action, if also for much else besides, told them, "If you love me, keep my commandments."

Appendix A: Other Christian Nationalisms

Americans are not alone in the world in their belief that God has singled out their nation for special divine prerogatives. The kind of claims that are made about America's special relationship with God have also been made at various times in recent centuries by the Dutch, by Germans, by Russians, and by citizens of other European countries. Such claims continue to reverberate with special effect from Calvinists in the Republic of South Africa and from Catholics in Poland, two modern nations that have experienced unusual stress in recent years. The pattern by which belief in a unique divine purpose developed in these two nations offers an instructive comparison with similar development in the United States.

In each of the three nations, a strong sense of national destiny under God is deeply rooted in history. For Americans, the Puritan "errand into the wilderness" first established the idea. New England, in the famous words of the first governor of Massachusetts, John Winthrop, would be "a city on a hill" because of its separate covenant with God.

During the War for Independence, as we have seen, American believers often recorded their belief that God was uniquely on their side. In 1781 the Congregationalist minister Moses Mather expatiated on the theme at considerable length: "The over-ruling hand of divine providence has been often so conspicuous in the events of the present war, as to extort a confession, even from infidelity itself, that it is God that fighteth for us."[1] The conviction of America's divine role grew during the nineteenth century, as religious leaders took note of how America's revivalists and missionaries were spreading the gospel far and wide. Political leaders likewise sang the praises of the rising tide of democracy in directly religious tones. America's successful liberation from Europe and the nation's burgeoning material prosperity strengthened the notion of special divine benevolence.

We are currently witnessing a striking resurgence of belief in God's special dealing with America. The preacher in what Teddy Roosevelt once called a bully pulpit affirmed in 1982 "that this anointed land was set apart in an uncommon way, that a divine plan placed this great continent here between the oceans to be found by people from every corner of the Earth who had a special love of faith and freedom."[2] Despite the rising assaults of secularization, the presence of freedom and faith in abundance has seemed to be proof of a special divine seal on the United States.

In South Africa early Dutch settlers brought with them a dynamic convenantal theology not untouched by convictions about Europe's special role in the divine economy.[3] It was, however, the great success, against overwhelming odds, of the *trek* by Boers from the Cape Colony into the Transvaal and the Orange Free State, 1836–1840, that confirmed that people in their belief in God's special providence on their behalf.

In both the United States and the Republic of South Africa, the sense of national messianism has been a two-edged sword. It has provided great energy for subduing a land (physically and culturally) for Christ. And it has played a part in the significant leadership that believers from both countries have exercised in the worldwide missionary effort. It has also led to the cultivation of a set of laudable personality traits, especially self-discipline, hard work, and purposeful energy.

But the cost of national messianism has also been great. In America, it was a factor in the brutal displacement of the Indians, in the blinding of American patriots to illegal treatment of Loyalists and Pacifists during the Revolutionary War, and in the heinous oppression of blacks, which intensified after the formation of the new nation. Whatever good may be said about convictions of special blessing, they also undergird a fair measure of the specious moral posturing that affects American policy abroad and at home. Though one must never deny the rich ingathering that the Word of God has reaped in the United States, it is also true that assumptions about a special national blessing have regularly contaminated the harvest.

In South Africa, national messianism has contributed its full measure to the development of that nation's enduring racialism. It also may be a factor in the diplomatic stubbornness that has characterized South Africa's relations with the rest of the world for several decades. In recent years a wide variety of interests outside South Africa and a growing chorus of Christian voices within have urged heirs of the *vortrekkers* to reconsider their messianic pretensions. But it survives as a mainstay of the racist sin that throughout the world blots the name of Calvin and, more importantly, of Christ.

In Poland, messianism has worked out differently, and it is instructive to see why. It seems that Polish messianism has never developed the evil effects to be seen in the United States and South Africa primarily because it has never been joined to the full exercise of political power. No less than Christian nationalists in America or South Africa, however, Christian nationalists in this Eastern European country believe that God has made an extraordinary covenant with their nation. It is not surprising that in an intensely Catholic country this conviction takes a Marian form. According to George Williams, Polish Catholics believe that their land sustains "a kind of heavenly nuptial covenant" with the Virgin Mary.[4]

The Counter-Reformation, which recaptured Poland for Rome, provides the deep historical background for Polish Christian nationalism. It took definite shape, however, only after a beleaguered Polish remnant triumphed miraculously in 1655 over the rampaging Swedes at the icon of the Virgin at the Paulite Monastery of Jasna Gora above the town of Czestochowa. Poland's messianic consciousness grew as the nation suffered the devastating blows that over the last several centuries have repeatedly wrenched its borders, subjected it to conquest, occupation, and economic prostration, and robbed it of everything except its common language and its Catholic faith. The messianism became more intense during the nineteenth century when Polish Catholics criticized the cold formalism of their own church and longed for a day of divine liberation, for a day when the suffering children of God could show the way to those grown fat with ease, for a day when, in the words of the poet Juliusz Slowacki,

Amid discord God strikes
At a bell immense,
For a Slavic Pope

He opened the throne . . .
Behold the Slavic Pope is coming,
A brother of the people.

A son of this suffering faith is now the pope, and the longing of the nineteenth-century poem is fulfilled. Even more remarkably, a vigorous Catholic church flourishes in an officially atheistic Poland. And out from under this Polish rubble are emerging—most visibly in the words of John Paul II—startlingly Christian visions of economic justice, family wholeness, evangelistic zeal, and social reconciliation. Only a little investigation is necessary, moreover, to discover that the pope's pronouncements are securely rooted in the Christian traditions that have matured in his native land. At least some of this Christian vigor may be accounted for by the fact that Poles hold tightly to their belief that God is using them to bring his light to the whole world. It is not surprising that their brother in Peter's chair, who wears an *M* for Mary on his papal crest beneath the cross of Christ, encourages special reverence for the Queen of Heaven, whom he first came to know as the Queen of Poland.

On the surface these Christian nationalisms look very different. Americans and South Africans strangle a sturdy evangelical gospel and mock the ethics of Jesus in part because they tolerate a Christian nationalism. Poles embody the gospel (despite defects that Protestants may find in its Catholic expression) and *advance* the ethics of Jesus in part because they embrace a Christian nationalism. The Poles may not be any more correct in their national messianism than the Americans or the South Africans, but at least that messianism has become for them a means of faithful Christian service.

A reason for the difference must certainly be the possession of power. American Protestants and South African Calvinists have had it; the Poles have not. A sense of divine mission—even if theologically incorrect—may still work for the good when a church is oppressed. But when such ideas are used to allow domination over other peoples in a civilization, the effects are skewed the other way. Communal suffering in the name of Christ may be the elixir that transforms the dross of Christian nationalism into the gold of Christian fidelity.

Appendix B: Limitations of the Constitution

One way of keeping evaluation of the Constitution in perspective is to cite the shrewd opinion of Walter Bagehot, a British contemporary of William Gladstone. Bagehot was only mildly impressed with the American Constitution, which he thought much inferior to Britain's system. To Bagehot the Constitution was a relatively confused instrument of government. It so divided principles of sovereignty as to invite chaos or the crafty manipulation of government by backstage operators. Bagehot admitted that the United States had enjoyed unrivaled prosperity in the nineteenth century and had set lofty standards for personal freedom. Yet the secret of America's success was not the Constitution, but the quality of people who lived under the Constitution. Said Bagehot in 1890: "The Americans now extol their institutions, and so defraud themselves of their due praise. But if they had not a genius for politics; if they had not a moderation in action singularly curious where superficial speech is so violent; if they had not a regard for law, such as no great people has yet evinced, and infinitely surpassing ours,—the multiplicity of authorities in the American Constitution would long ago have brought it to a bad end."[1]

Bagehot was arguing that the instrument of government was less important for the well-being of a state than the character of its people. His observation is not entirely at odds with the founders' own convictions. Nevertheless, it also suggests questions about the relationship that the founding fathers established between their own moral assumptions and the government they established.

The Constitution was written by people who held to a more or less Christian morality. Among the founders, even the deists or the worshipers of the Christ-less God of Nature upheld a positive morality largely compatible with Christian values. Thomas Jefferson is perhaps the best example. He had abandoned belief in the supernatural character and mission of Jesus, but he was still devoted to "The Life and Morals of Jesus" (as he called one of his two abridgments of the New Testament). As a consequence, Jefferson the deist conducted himself as secretary of state, vice president, and president with dignity, scrupulous honesty, and an altruistic dedication to the well-being of the commonwealth. Although he was not a Christian in the traditional sense of the word, his character manifested a high order of "Christian" morality. What was true for Jefferson was even truer for many of his contemporaries. When they thought of public virtue, public justice, or public responsibilities, they thought in terms informed by Christian assumptions.

Precisely at this point, however, a difficulty arises. Christian morality may have been a common assumption of the founding generation, but the language of the Constitution was the language of experience and science. As the delegates to the Philadelphia convention and the state ratifying conventions debated the new Constitution, their frame of reference was experience. What had happened under the British to abridge liberty? Where had the new states swung too far in promoting "the will of the people"? How might the Constitution rectify abuses of power witnessed over the past forty years?

The other explicit guide was "the science of politics," a phrase that both Madison and Hamilton used in *The Federalist Papers*. In this respect the American founding fathers showed that they were participating wholeheartedly in the eighteenth-century Enlightenment, the movement drawing inspiration from Newton's discoveries in nature and going on confidently to apply scientific understanding to society. "The science of politics" showed Madison that a large republic might work where small ones failed. It told Hamilton that a modern nation needed sound fiscal management if it were to gain the respect of other nations.

The difficulty with resting so heavily on experience and "the science of politics" was a difficulty for the future more than for the time of the Constitution itself. The founders' "science of politics" was put to use in a social setting in which the dominant assumptions about public virtue and political morality were more or less Christian. In addition, they acted in a political setting in which the primary motivation was to prevent the repetition of past evils. Consequently, several important conclusions about politics in general, and about the nature of the United States government in particular, were left in limbo.

At least three problems resulted. First, the Constitution's debt to "experience" showed most damagingly in its toleration of slavery. Some of the founders were prepared to work for a constitution prohibiting slavery, at least at a specified date in the future, but practical politics got in the way. Representatives from slave states would not tolerate any national attack on "the peculiar institution." Perhaps there could have been no new nation without toleration of slavery. In any event, expedience won out over principle, and the nation has suffered ever since.

Second, the Constitution contained little consideration of the positive role of government. It was an admirable instrument for preventing dangerous accumulations of power (and in this regard partook of a Christian spirit). It was less successful in stating the positive purposes of the state. European and American Christians had proposed many such theories before 1787, and several varieties of believers have offered a number of possibilities since. A common theme in many Christian theories about the positive purpose of government is that government should ensure justice for all citizens and should also broker fairness in the public square. That is, because God has created the state to act on behalf of all people, the state must promote the human dignity that God through the creation bestowed on all people as individuals and all people in their social groups. But this sort of purpose is present only implicitly in the Constitution. For the slaves in early America, it was absent altogether.

A third issue concerns the relationship of the Constitution to the values of United States citizens. The founders relied upon traditional, largely Christian values as a framework for the Constitution. They did not, however, address the question of how the Constitution was to function if the supporting culture changed. By defining itself so closely as an instrument to protect individual liberties, and avoiding the issue of where those liberties were rooted, the Constitution possessed no real means to check trends that might bring about a society in which those assumptions about natural rights were no longer accepted. Although the Constitution made it difficult for the whim of the moment to change the law, in the end it was dependent upon the will of the people. As a protection of individual liberties, this was all to the good. Both before 1787 and since, the world has witnessed a parade of horrors perpetrated by rulers who felt they had some kind of divine, natural, or historical right to rule without popular consent. At the same time, because of failure to root concepts of liberty and freedom in some larger philosophy (e.g., that individuals have rights because God has made people in his image), the meaning of crucial constitutional concepts like "freedom" and "liberty" always remain subject to majority opinion, or to the opinion of those who exploit the majority to secure their own power.

So long as the values of the culture in which the Constitution functioned did not change greatly, the absence of explicit statements on these points was not a major problem. Christian ideas of justice, though never entirely dominant in early America, were nonetheless an accepted part of the cultural landscape. The day would come, however, when the residual Christianity faded in American culture, when both "experience" and "the science of politics" harkened to impulses alien to the Christian faith. When that day arrived, the intuitive character of the Constitution became a bane instead of the substantial blessing it had been in its own generation.

But would it have made a difference if the founders had acknowledged that rights and liberties come from the will of God instead of from nature or the will of the people? Maybe and maybe not. Since they did not, contemporary Christians need to treat the Constitution for what it is instead of what it is not. The Constitution is a good, even noble, instrument of government, but it is not a Christian frame of government as such. In addition, the founders chose to incorporate very little of their political philosophy in the document. The result seems to have been a conscious choice of the founders: the touchstone of our national lives today remains the Constitution itself, not the substantially Christian frame of reference in which it was written.[2]

Notes

INTRODUCTION

1. Mark A. Noll, George Marsden, and Nathan Hatch, *The Search for Christian America* (Westchester, IL: Crossway Books, 1983).
2. Thankfully, there are many exceptions to that generalization, of which the following have been especially helpful to me: Harold O. J. Brown, *The Reconstruction of the Republic*, rev. ed. (Milford, MI: Mott Media, 1981); John P. Diggins, *The Lost Soul of American Politics: Virtue, Self-Interest, and the Foundations of Liberalism* (New York: Basic Books, 1984); James Turner Johnson, ed., *The Bible in American Law, Politics, and Political Rhetoric* (Philadelphia: Fortress, 1985); H. M. Kuitert, *Everything Is Politics But Politics Is Not Everything* (Grand Rapids: Eerdmans, 1986); Martin E. Marty, *A Nation of Behavers* (Chicago: University of Chicago Press, 1976); William Lee Miller, *The First Liberty: Religion and the American Republic* (New York: Knopf, 1985); Richard J. Mouw, *Political Evangelism* (Grand Rapids: Eerdmans, 1974); Richard J. Neuhaus, *The Naked Public Square* (Grand Rapids: Eerdmans, 1984); A. James Reichley, *Religion in American Public Life* (Washington, DC: The Brookings Institution, 1985); James W. Skillen, ed., *Confessing Christ and Doing Politics* (Washington, DC: Association for Public Justice Education Fund, 1982); Nicholas Wolterstorff, *Until Justice and Peace Embrace* (Grand Rapids: Eerdmans, 1983). Works that have shaped my thinking on the subject of this book, but that stand further in the background, both chronologically and conceptually, are H. Richard Niebuhr, *The Kingdom of God in America* (New York: Harper & Row, 1937); and *Christ and Culture* (New York: Harper & Row, 1951); and Reinhold Niebuhr, *The Irony of American History* (New York: Charles Scribner's Sons, 1952).
3. An especially important passage in Scripture for such an assertion is the discussion of the state in Romans 13. In that passage, the statement in verse 4 that the ruler is "God's servant" is particularly crucial, since the same word *(diakonos)* is used here of the ruler that is applied elsewhere in the New Testament to those who serve God in religious settings.
4. Chapter 10, "The Bible and Politics," develops this conviction at somewhat greater length, with some attention to biblical passages themselves.

CHAPTER 1: A "CHRISTIAN AMERICA"? NO AND YES

1. On the role of religion for the founding fathers, see *Religion and the American Revolution*, ed. Jerald C. Brauer (Philadelphia: Fortress, 1976); Mark A. Noll, "The Bible in Revolutionary America," in *The Bible in American Law, Politics, and Political Rhetoric*, ed. James Turner Johnson (Philadelphia: Fortress, 1985), 39–60; and Stephen Botein, "Religious Dimensions of the Early American State," in *Beyond Confederation: Origins*

of the Constitution and American National Identity, ed. Richard Beeman et al. (Chapel Hill: University of North Carolina Press, 1987).

CHAPTER 2: AMERICA'S "REFORMED" TRADITION

1. For an excellent overview of the subject, see A. G. Dickens, *The English Reformation* (New York: Schocken, 1964), and for a general survey of the main strands of Christian doctrine in the Reformation era, see Jaroslav Pelikan, *Reformation of Church and Dogma (1300–1700),* vol. 4 of *The Christian Tradition,* (Chicago: University of Chicago Press, 1984).

2. John Knox, quoted in John T. McNeill, *The History and Character of Calvinism* (New York: Oxford University Press, 1967), 178.

3. A fine essay comparing the theology of Luther and Calvin is Brian Gerrish, "John Calvin on Luther," in *Interpreters of Luther,* ed. Jaroslav Pelikan (Philadelphia: Fortress, 1968).

4. W. Fred Graham, *The Constructive Revolutionary: John Calvin and His Socio-Economic Impact* (Atlanta: John Knox, 1971), 20–21.

5. On the power of this democratic ideology and its effects on religion in America, see Gordon S. Wood, "The Democratization of Mind in the American Revolution," in *The Moral Foundations of the American Republic,* ed. Robert H. Horwitz (Charlottesville: University Press of Virginia, 1979); and Nathan O. Hatch, "The Christian Movement and the Demand for a Theology of the People," *Journal of American History* 67 (1980), 545–67.

6. Sydney E. Ahlstrom, *A Religious History of the American People* (New Haven: Yale University Press, 1972), part 4.

7. H. Richard Niebuhr, *Christ and Culture* (New York: Harper & Row, 1951). This is a book of enduring value for its cataloguing of ideal types of the way that Christians have interacted with the world.

CHAPTER 3: THE AMERICAN REVOLUTION

1. For excellent general treatments of the development of republicanism, see J. G. A. Pocock, *The Machiavellian Moment: Florentine Political Thought and the Atlantic Republican Tradition* (Princeton: Princeton University Press, 1975); Caroline Robbins, *The Eighteenth-Century Commonwealthman* (Cambridge: Harvard University Press, 1959); and Bernard Bailyn, *The Ideological Origins of the American Revolution* (Cambridge: Harvard University Press, 1967).

2. *The Founders' Constitution,* ed. Philip B. Kurland and Ralph Lerner, 5 vols. (Chicago: University of Chicago Press, 1987), 1:97.

3. Ibid.

4. *Documents of American History,* ed. Henry Steele Commager, 2 vols., 8th ed. (New York: Appleton-Century-Crofts, 1968), 2:60–61.

5. For further discussion of these similarities, see Mark A. Noll, *Christians in the American Revolution* (Grand Rapids: Eerdmans, 1977), 52–57.

6. Edmund S. Morgan, *The Birth of the Republic, 1763–1789* (Chicago: University of Chicago Press, 1956), 6.

7. On Mayhew's sermon and its effects, see Bernard Bailyn, "Religion and Revolution: Three Biographical Sketches," *Perspectives in American History* 4 (1970), 111 ff.

8. See Edmund S. Morgan, "The Puritan Ethic and the American Revolution," *William and Mary Quarterly* 24 (Jan. 1967), 3–43.

9. See Harry S. Stout, *The New England Soul: Preaching and Religious Culture in Colonial New England* (New York: Oxford University press, 1986).

10. Quoted in Patricia U. Bonomi, *Under the Cope of Heaven: Religion, Society, and Politics in Colonial America* (New York: Oxford University Press, 1986), 210.

11. The service rendered by religion to the American Revolution is well catalogued in Bonomi, *Under the Cope of Heaven;* Alan Heimert, *Religion and the American Mind from the Great Awakening to the Revolution* (Cambridge: Harvard University Press, 1966); Alice M. Baldwin, *The New England Clergy and the American Revolution* (Durham, NC: Duke University Press, 1928); Nathan O. Hatch, *The Sacred Cause of Liberty: Republican Thought and the Millennium in Revolutionary New England* (New Haven: Yale University Press, 1977); John F. Berens, *Providence and Patriotism in Early America, 1640–1815* (Charlottesville: University Press of Virginia, 1978); and Noll, *Christians in the American Revolution.*

12. Quoted in Leonard J. Kramer, "Muskets in the Pulpit, 1776–1783," *Journal of the Presbyterian Historical Society* 31 (1953), 320.

13. Quoted in Kramer, "Presbyterians Approach the American Revolution," ibid., 176.

14. Bonomi, *Under the Cope of Heaven,* 216.

15. Quoted in Edmund S. Morgan, *The Gentle Puritan: A Life of Ezra Stiles, 1727–1795* (Chapel Hill: University of North Carolina Press, 1962), 262–63.

16. Samuel Sherwood, *The Church's Flight into the Wilderness* (New York: S. Loudon, 1776), 14–15; Samuel West, *A Sermon Preached Before the Honorable Council* (Boston: John Gill, 1776), 63.

17. Sherwood, *The Church's Flight,* 14–15.

18. Samuel Davies, *The Crisis,* in *Sermons on Important Subjects* (Philadelphia, 1818), 5:257–58.

19. Quoted in Oscar Zeichner, *Connecticut's Years of Controversy, 1750–1776* (Chapel Hill: University of North Carolina Press, 1949), 51, 74.

20. Quoted in William C. Fowler, "The Ministers of Connecticut in the Revolution," *Centennial Papers, Published by order of the Congregational Churches of Connecticut* (Hartford: Case, Lockwood & Brainard, 1877), 35.

21. Abraham Keteltas, *God Arising and Pleading His People's Cause; or, the American War in favor of Liberty, against . . . Great Britain, shewn to be the Cause of God* (Newburyport, MA: John Mycall, 1777), 27, 30.

22. Robert Smith, *The Obligations of the Confederate States of North America to Praise God* (Philadelphia: Francis Bailey, 1782), 33. Some of the many other sermons of this sort are included in the bibliographies and notes of Hatch, *The Sacred Cause of Liberty;* Baldwin, *The New England Clergy;* and Berens, *Providence and Patriotism.*

23. Clifford K. Shipton, *Sibley's Harvard Graduates,* vols. 4–14 (Boston: Massachusetts Historical Society, 1933–1968), 13:47–60.

24. Kramer, "Presbyterians Approach the Revolution," 171.

25. Jonathan Edwards, *The Nature of True Virtue* (1765).

26. Samuel Hopkins, *A Dialogue Concerning the Slavery of the Africans* (Norwich, CT: Judah P. Spooner, 1776), 30.

27. See Harry S. Stout, "Religion, Communications, and the Ideological Origins of the American Revolution," *William and Mary Quarterly,* 3d ser., 34 (1977), 519–41.

CHAPTER 4: THEORY, COMPROMISE, AND THE CONSTITUTION

1. For general coverage, see Merrill Jensen, *The New Nation: A History of the United States During the Confederation, 1781–1789* (New York: Knopf, 1950); Gordon S. Wood, ed., *The Confederation and the Constitution: The Critical Issues* (Boston: Little, Brown, 1973); and Richard Beeman, et al., ed., *Beyond Confederation: Origins of the Constitution and American National Identity* (Chapel Hill: University of North Carolina Press, 1987).

2. These are detailed in Edward S. Corwin, "The Progress of Constitutional Theory Between the Declaration of Independence and the Meeting of the Philadelphia Convention," in Wood, ed., *The Confederation and the Constitution,* 18.

3. Ruth Bloch, *Visionary Republic: Millennial Themes in American Thought, 1756–1800* (New York: Cambridge University Press, 1985), 102.

4. Quoted in Gordon S. Wood, *The Creation of the American Republic, 1776–1787* (Chapel Hill: University of North Carolina Press, 1969), 427–28.

5. A good short record of the Constitution is found in Michael Kammen, ed., *The Origins of the American Constitution: A Documentary History* (New York: Penguin, 1986); a nearly definitive account is provided by *The Founders' Constitution,* ed. Philip B. Kurland and Ralph Lerner, 5 vols. (Chicago: University of Chicago Press, 1987).

6. *Founders' Constitution,* 1:673.

7. John Woodhull, *A Sermon, for the Day of Publick Thanksgiving* (Trenton: Isaac Collins, 1790), 23.

8. *Founders' Constitution,* 5:48.

9. Ibid., 4:634.

10. Ibid., 5:103.

11. Ibid., 4:635.

12. Ibid., 4:638–39.

13. These questions are probed at greater length in Mark A. Noll, Nathan O. Hatch, and George M. Marsden, *The Search for Christian America* (Westchester, IL: Crossway Books, 1983), 95–100.

14. *The Mind of the Founder: Sources of the Political Thought of James Madison,* ed. Marvin Meyers, rev. ed. (Hanover, NH: Brandeis University Press, 1981), 88–95.

15. Sydney E. Ahlstrom, *A Religious History of the American People* (New Haven: Yale University Press, 1972), 387 ff.

16. For a range of perspectives on the revivalistic impulse, see Donald G. Mathews, "The Second Great Awakening as an Organizing Process, 1780–1830," *American Quarterly* 21 (1969), 23–43; Paul E. Johnson, *A Shopkeeper's Millennium: Society and Revivals in Rochester, New York, 1815–1837* (New York: Hill and Wang, 1978); and Timothy L. Smith, "Righteousness and Hope: Christian Holiness and the Millennial Vision in America, 1800–1900," *American Quarterly* 31 (1979), 32–45.

17. For example, Fred J. Hood, *Reformed America: The Middle and Southern States, 1783–1837* (University, AL: University of Alabama Press, 1980).

18. *Founders' Constitution,* 5:106.
19. Lyman Beecher, *Autobiography,* ed. Barbara M. Cross, 2 vols. (Cambridge: Harvard University Press, 1961), vol. 1.
20. *Founders' Constitution,* 5:108.

CHAPTER 5: THE CAMPAIGN OF 1800

1. Thomas Jefferson, *"Notes on the State of Virginia,"* from *Jefferson* (New York: The Library of America, 1984), 285–87. For an outstanding biography of Jefferson that is also a splendid account of his times, see Dumas Malone, *Jefferson and His Time,* 6 vols. (Boston: Little, Brown, 1948–1981).
2. Reliable general works on the 1790s and Jefferson's administration are John C. Miller, *The Federalist Era, 1789–1801* (New York: Harper & Brothers, 1960); and Marshall Smelser, *The Democratic Republic, 1801–1815* (New York: Harper & Row, 1968).
3. Timothy Dwight, *The Duty of Americans at the Present Crisis, Illustrated in the Discourse, Preached on the Fourth of July 1798* (New Haven: Thomas and Samuel Green, 1798), as quoted in Fred C. Luebke, "The Origins of Thomas Jefferson's Anti-Clericalism," *Church History* 32 (1963), 346.
4. John Mitchell Mason, *The Voice of Warning to Christians on the Ensuing Election of a President of the United States* (1800), from *The Complete Works of John Mitchell Mason,* vol. 4 (New York: Baker and Scribner, 1849), 537.
5. William Linn, *Serious Considerations on the Election of a President, Addressed to the Citizens of the United States* (New York: John Furman, 1800).
6. *Gazette of the United States,* quoted in Merrill D. Peterson, *Thomas Jefferson and the New Nation* (New York: Oxford University Press, 1970), 638.
7. *Acts and Proceedings of the General Assembly of the Presbyterian Church in the United States of America, May 11, 1798* (Philadelphia: Presbyterian Church, 1798), 11.
8. See Vernon Stauffer, *New England and the Bavarian Illuminati* (New York: Columbia University Press, 1918).
9. Elias Boudinot, quoted in George Adams Boyd, *Elias Boudinot: Patriot and Statesman 1740–1821* (Princeton: Princeton University Press, 1952), 239.
10. Samuel Stanhope Smith to Jonathan Dayton, Dec. 22, 1801, in Samuel Stanhope Smith Papers, Princeton University Library.
11. Elias Boudinot to Elisha Boudinot, Jan. 7, 1801, in Thorne Boudinot Collection, Princeton University Library.
12. John Cosens Ogden, *A View of the New England Illuminati: who are indefatigably engaged in destroying the religion and government of the United States; under a feigned regard for their safety—and under an impious abuse of true religion* (Philadelphia: James Carey, 1799).
13. Benjamin Rush to Thomas Jefferson, Oct. 6, 1800, in *Jefferson's Extracts from the Gospels,* ed. Dickinson W. Adams, *The Papers of Thomas Jefferson: Second Series* (Princeton: Princeton University Press, 1983), 321–22.
14. "Consociation Records, Hartford North Association, 1790–1820," Congregational Library, Hartford, Conn., 136; as quoted in David William Kling, "Clergy and Society in the Second Great Awakening in Connecticut" (Ph.D. diss., University of Chicago, 1986), 51–52.
15. Thomas Jefferson to William Baldwin, Jan. 19, 1810, in *Jefferson's Extracts from the Gospels,* 345.
16. Ibid.

CHAPTER 6: THE TRANSCENDENT FAITH OF ABRAHAM LINCOLN

1. J. G. Randall and Richard N. Current, *Lincoln the President: Last Full Measure* (New York: Dodd, Mead, 1955), 375.
2. Many of the statements about Lincoln's religion in this chapter rely upon William J. Wolf, *The Almost Chosen People: A Study of the Religion of Abraham Lincoln* (Garden City, NY: Doubleday, 1959).
3. Roy P. Basler, ed., *The Collected Works of Abraham Lincoln,* 9 vols. (New Brunswick: Rutgers University Press, 1953), 1:382.
4. Benjamin Thomas, *Abraham Lincoln* (New York: Knopf, 1952); Stephen B. Oates, *With Malice Toward None: The Life of Abraham Lincoln* (New York: Harper & Row, 1977); James Garfield Randall, *Lincoln the President,* 4 vols. (New York: Dodd, Mead, 1946–1955); Stephen B. Oates, *Abraham Lincoln: The Man Behind the Myths* (New York: Harper & Row, 1984). After Wolf, *The Almost Chosen People,* a helpful study on Lincoln's religion is Hans J. Morgenthau and David Hein, *Essays on Lincoln's Faith and Politics,* ed. Kenneth W. Thompson (Lanham, MD: University Press of America, 1983).
5. Lewis O. Saum, *The Popular Mood of Pre–Civil War America* (Westport, CT: Greenwood, 1980), xxiii.
6. Lincoln, quoted in Wolf, *The Almost Chosen People,* 86.
7. *Collected Works,* 7:542.
8. Ibid., 6:39.
9. Lincoln, quoted in Oates, *Abraham Lincoln: The Man Behind the Myths,* 151–52.
10. Frederick Douglass, quoted in ibid., 107.
11. Martin E. Marty, "Two Kinds of Civil Religion," in *American Civil Religion,* ed. Russell E. Richey and Donald G. Jones (New York: Harper & Row, 1974), 47–49.
12. *Collected Works,* 2:501.
13. Ibid., 4:270–71.
14. Ibid., 6:114–15.
15. Ibid., 6:155–56.
16. Ibid., 5:404n.
17. Ibid., 5:403–4.
18. Ibid., 8:333.
19. Samuel Hopkins, *A Dialogue Concerning the Slavery of the Africans* (Norwich, CT: Judah P. Spooner, 1776), 21.
20. *Collected Works,* 6:535–36.

CHAPTER 7: ABOLITION

1. See James D. Essig, *The Bonds of Wickedness: American Evangelicals Against Slavery, 1770–1808* (Philadelphia: Temple University Press, 1982).
2. The best biographical study is Keith J. Hardman, *Charles Grandison Finney, 1792–1875: Revivalist and Reformer* (Syracuse: Syracuse University Press, 1987).
3. Quoted in ibid., 85.
4. Ibid., 25.

5. Ronald G. Walters, *American Reformers 1815–1860* (New York: Hill and Wang, 1978), 23.

6. John Humphrey Noyes, quoted in Bernard Bailyn et al., *The Great Republic: A History of the American People,* 2 vols. (Boston: D. C. Heath, 1977), 1:532.

7. Charles G. Finney, *Lectures on Revivals of Religion* (New York: Fleming H. Revell, 1886), 282–86.

8. A good biography is Robert H. Abzug, *Passionate Liberator: Theodore Dwight Weld and the Dilemma of Reform* (New York: Oxford University Press, 1980).

9. Theodore Dwight Weld, quoted in James Brewer Stewart, *Holy Warriors: The Abolitionists and American Slavery* (New York: Hill and Wang, 1976), 43.

10. William Lloyd Garrison, quoted in John L. Thomas, *The Liberator: William Lloyd Garrison* (Boston: Little, Brown, 1963), 65.

11. Garrison, quoted in Walters, *American Reformers,* 79.

12. Garrison, quoted in Thomas, *William Lloyd Garrison,* 128.

13. Elijah Lovejoy, quoted in Louis Filler, *The Crusade Against Slavery, 1830–1860* (New York: Harper & Brothers, 1960), 80.

14. Albert Barnes, *An Inquiry into the Scriptural Views of Slavery* (Philadelphia: Perkins & Purves, 1846), 340.

15. Ibid., 355, 357, 375.

16. Frederick Ross, quoted in Eugene D. Genovese, *"Slavery Ordained of God": The Southern Slaveholders' View of Biblical History and Modern Politics* (Gettysburg, Pa: Gettysburg College, 1985), 19.

17. Howell Cobb, *A Scriptural Examination of the Institution of Slavery* (Georgia: by the author, 1856), 9.

18. J. Blanchard and N. L. Rice, *A Debate on Slavery* (Cincinnati: Moore, Wilstach, Keys, 1857 [orig. 1846]), 291.

19. See C. C. Goen, *Broken Churches, Broken Nation: Denominational Schism and the Coming of the Civil War* (Macon, GA: Mercer University Press, 1985).

20. Finney, *Lectures on Revivals,* 281.

21. There are good accounts of the Liberty Party in Filler, *The Crusade Against Slavery;* and Stewart, *Holy Warriors.*

22. Finney, quoted in Hardman, *Charles Grandison Finney,* 370.

23. Lawrence Thomas Lesick, *The Lane Rebels: Evangelicalism and Antislavery in Antebellum America* (Metuchen, NJ: Scarecrow, 1980), 199.

24. Abzug, *Theodore Dwight Weld,* 246–47.

25. Garrison, quoted in Thomas, *William Lloyd Garrison,* 352.

26. *Encyclopedia of the American Constitution,* ed. Leonard W. Levy (New York: Macmillan, 1986), 2:835.

27. See Leon F. Litwack, *North of Slavery: The Negro in the Free States, 1790–1860* (Chicago: University of Chicago Press, 1961); and Stewart, *Holy Warriors, passim.*

CHAPTER 8: PROHIBITION

1. For a wealth of information on drinking in early New England, see Gerald Carson, *Rum and Reform in Old New England* (Sturbridge, MA: Old Sturbridge Village, 1966).

2. Increase Mather, quoted in W. J. Rorabaugh, *The Alcoholic Republic: An American Tradition* (New York: Oxford University Press, 1979), 23.

3. For good general overviews, see Norman H. Clark, *Deliver Us from Evil: An Interpretation of American Prohibition* (New York: W. W. Norton, 1976); and Joseph R. Gusfield, *Symbolic Crusade: Status Politics and the American Temperance Movement* (Urbana: University of Illinois Press, 1963).

4. Rorabaugh, *Alcoholic Republic,* 233.

5. Ibid., 20–21.

6. *The Autobiography of Lyman Beecher,* ed. Barbara M. Cross, 2 vols. (Cambridge: Harvard University Press, 1961), 1:179–80.

7. Ronald Walters, *American Reformers 1815–1860* (New York: Hill and Wang, 1978), 123.

8. Lyman Beecher, *Six Sermons,* (New York: American Tract Society, 1843), 38.

9. Benjamin P. Thomas, *Abraham Lincoln* (New York: Knopf, 1952), 37.

10. Thomas Laurie, "What Wine Shall We Use at the Lord's Supper?" *Bibliotheca Sacra* 26 (1869), 182.

11. G. W. Samson, *Cyclopedia of Temperance and Prohibition* (New York: Funk & Wagnalls, 1891), 55–56.

12. William Thayer, *Communion Wine and Bible Temperance: Being a Review of Dr. Thos. Laurie's Article* (New York: National Temperance Society, 1869), 4–5.

13. George Duffield, *The Bible Rule of Temperance: Total Abstinence from All Intoxicating Drink* (New York: National Temperance Society, 1868), 10, 17–18.

14. Rorabaugh, *Alcoholic Republic,* 233; the figure drops to 1.8 gallons in 1850, perhaps reflecting the political success of the temperance reformers.

15. Svend Petersen, *A Statistical History of the American Presidential Elections* (New York: Frederick Unger, 1963), table 47.

16. Walters, *American Reformers,* 138.

17. Clark, *Deliver Us from Evil,* 137–39.

18. Billy Sunday, quoted in Herbert Asbury, *The Great Illusion: An Informal History of Prohibition* (Westport, CT: Greenwood, 1968), 144–45.

CHAPTER 9: THE LESSONS OF HISTORY

1. See William G. McLoughlin, *Cherokees and Missionaries* (New Haven: Yale University Press, 1984).

2. See Ray Allen Billington, *The Protestant Crusade, 1800–1860: A Study of the Origins of American Nativism* (New York: Macmillan, 1938).

3. See Ronald C. White, Jr., and C. Howard Hopkins, *The Social Gospel: Religion and Reform in Changing America* (Philadelphia: Temple University Press, 1976).

4. On Woodrow Wilson's religious context, see John M. Mulder, *Woodrow Wilson: The Years of Preparation* (Princeton: Princeton University Press, 1978); and for an excellent general study, Arthur S. Link, *Woodrow Wilson,* 3 vols. to date (Princeton: Princeton University Press, 1947–).

5. See Lawrence W. Levine, *Defender of the Faith: William Jennings Bryan: The Last Decade* (New York: Oxford University Press, 1965); and Paolo E. Coletta, *William Jennings Bryan,* 3 vols. (Lincoln: University of Nebraska Press, 1964–1969).

6. *William Jennings Bryan: Selections,* ed. Ray Ginger (Indianapolis: Bobbs-Merrill, 1967), 46.
7. For an excellent biography, see Edmund S. Morgan, *The Puritan Dilemma: The Story of John Winthrop* (Boston: Little, Brown, 1958).
8. Eric Foner, ed., *The Life and Writings of Frederick Douglass,* 2:64, as quoted in Leon F. Litwack, *North of Slavery: The Negro in the Free States, 1790–1860* (Chicago: University of Chicago Press, 1961), 243.
9. A good biographical study is John Pollock, *Wilberforce* (London: Constable, 1977).
10. For example, from Martin E. Marty, "Two Kind of Two Kinds of Civil Religion," *American Civil Religion,* ed. Russell E. Richey and Donald G. Jones (New York: Harper & Row, 1974); and Robert N. Bellah, *The Broken Covenant: American Civil Religion in Time of Trial* (New York: Seabury, 1975).

CHAPTER 10: THE BIBLE AND POLITICS

1. On the particular place of the Bible with respect to American political assumptions, see Nathan O. Hatch, *"Sola Scriptura* and *Novus Ordo Seclorum,"* in *The Bible in America,* ed. Nathan O. Hatch and Mark A. Noll (New York: Oxford University Press, 1982).
2. Benjamin Trumbull, *A Discourse* (New Haven, CT: Thomas & Samuel Green, 1773).
3. The sermon was by David Ramsay of Charleston, South Carolina; see "David Ramsay," in *Princetonians 1748–1768: A Biographical Dictionary,* ed. James McLachlan (Princeton: Princeton University Press, 1976), 518.
4. Benjamin N. Palmer, *National Responsibility Before God* (New Orleans, 1861), 5; as quoted in James W. Silver, *Confederate Morale and Church Propaganda* (Gloucester, MA: Peter Smith, 1964 [orig. 1957]), 27.
5. John H. Leith, ed., *Creeds of the Churches* 3d ed. (Atlanta: John Knox, 1982), 267, 193.

CHAPTER 11: THE CHALLENGE TODAY

1. For perceptive comments on how the church might better stand over against the world, see George Marsden, "Let the Church Be a Sect," *Reformed Journal,* Feb. 1987, 2–3.
2. The texts in this paragraph are from Mark 8:36, NIV, Matt. 22:21; 22:39; 25:40; and John 14:15, KJV.

APPENDIX A: OTHER CHRISTIAN NATIONALISMS

1. Moses Mather, *Election Sermon* (New London, CT: Timothy Green, 1781), 16.
2. Ronald Reagan, quoted in K. L. Woodward, "How The Bible Made America," *Newsweek,* Dec. 27, 1982, p. 44.
3. For background, see J. Alton Templin, *Ideology on a Frontier: The Theological Foundations of Afrikaner Nationalism, 1652–1910* (Westport, CT: Greenwood, 1984).
4. George H. Williams, *The Mind of John Paul II* (New York: Seabury, 1981); this book offers outstanding general background on Catholicism in Poland as well as more specifically on the current pope.

APPENDIX B: LIMITATIONS OF THE CONSTITUTION

1. Walter Bagehot, *The English Constitution, and Other Political Essays* (New York: D. Appleton, 1890), 296.
2. For a discussion of how that historical situation influences interpretations of the Constitution today, see Stephen Botein, "Religious Dimensions of the Early American State," in *Beyond Confederation: Origins of the Constitution and American National Identity,* ed. Richard Beeman et al. (Chapel Hill: University of North Carolina Press, 1987).

Acknowledgments

Several chapters in this book include revised versions of articles, or parts of articles, published over the last several years. For their help in bringing out those earlier essays I would like to thank several editors: Clif Orlebeke of the *Christian Scholar's Review* ("From the Great Awakening to the American Revolution: Christian Values in the American Revolution," 12 [1983]; "Christian and Humanistic Values in Eighteenth-Century America," 6 [1976]); Jon Pott of the *Reformed Journal* ("The Paradox of Lincoln's Faith," Feb. 1985; "A Polish Irony," Oct. 1983); Rodney Clapp, Tom Minnery, Harold Myra, and Harold Smith at *Christianity Today* ("The Constitution at 200: Should Christians Join the Celebration?" July 10, 1987; "Is This Land God's Land?" July 11, 1986; "The Perplexing Faith of Abraham Lincoln," Feb. 15, 1985; "When 'Infidels' Run for Office," Oct. 5, 1984; "America's Battle Against the Bottle," Jan. 19, 1979); Linda-Marie Delloff and Martin Marty of the *Christian Century* ("Reasons and Arguments in the Constitution," May 20–27, 1987); and Bryce Christensen of *Chronicles* ("Protestant Polities, Religion, and American Public Life," Sept. 1987). In every case, the essays have been thoroughly rewritten for this book. In addition, I have repeated here a very few quotations or matters of fact first used for other purposes in *The Bible in America,* which I edited with Nathan Hatch (Oxford, 1982), and *The Search for Christian America,* co-authored with Nathan Hatch and George Marsden (Crossway Books, 1983).

I would also like to express appreciation to my Wheaton colleague Lyle Dorsett for graciously taking time to check a nearly complete draft for errors of fact and interpretation; to Mrs. Beatrice Horne for superb service as a typist and office manager; to Joel Carpenter for handling so competently the work of Wheaton's Institute for the Study of American Evangelicals; to Bob Lackie who gave me carte blanche to use his good work on the presidential campaign of 1800; to the

Institute for Advanced Christian Study and the Pew Memorial Trusts, whose grants for another project also freed up some time to work on this book; to Jim Skillen, executive director of the Association of Public Justice, for a long history of fruitful instruction in matters political; to Nathan Hatch and George Marsden, patient collaborators who supply most of my good ideas; to my wife, Maggie, and my children, Mary, David, and Robert Francis, for tolerating so graciously a historian with the scribbler's itch; and to the chairman of Wheaton's history department, Tom Kay, for providing space of several different kinds for academic work and popular writing.

General Index

Scripture Index

DATE DUE

FEB 2 8 1988		
MAR 1 7 1989		
FEB 2 1 1990		
OCT 0 3 1990		
OCT 19 1990		
NOV 2 0 1990		
FEB 0 9 1993		
MAR 0 1 1993		
APR 0 3 1996		
1-22-2000		
~~RESERVE~~		
~~JAN — 2000~~		
~~02 3/02~~		
NOV 0 1 2013		
GAYLORD		PRINTED IN U.S.A.